# PEOPLE'S PARTICIPATION IN SOIL AND WATER CONSERVATION THROUGH WATERSHED APPROACH

### G.L. Bagdi

Scientist (Sr. Scale),
(Agricultural Extension)
Central Soil and Water Conservation
Research and Training Institute, Research Centre,
Vasad-388 306, District Anand, Gujarat (India)

## International Book Distributing Co.

(Publishing Division)

*Published by*

**INTERNATIONAL BOOK DISTRIBUTING CO.**
(Publishing Division)
Chaman Studio Building, 2nd Floor,
Charbagh, Lucknow 226 004 U.P. (INDIA)
Tel. : Off. : 2450004, 2450007, 2459058  Fax : 0522-2458629
E-mail : ibdco@sancharnet.in

**First Edition 2005**

ISBN 81-8189-054-X

©Publisher
All Rights Reserved

No part of this publication may be reproduced, stored in a retrieval system or transmitted, in any form or by any means, electronic, mechanical, photocopying, recording or otherwise, without the prior written permission of the publisher.

*Laser Type Setting at :*
Tribhuwan Enterprises
Lucknow.  Mob.: 9415157635

*Printed at :*
Dewa Printers & Stationers
D-87/4, Indira Nagar,
Lucknow-226 016
Tel. : 0522-2343760, (M) 9415020896

# CONTENTS

| Sr. No. | CHAPTERS | Page No. |
|---|---|---|
| | Preface | 1-2 |
| 1. | **Soil and water conservation through watershed approach** | **3-10** |
| | 1.1 Watershed | 3 |
| | 1.2 Why Watershed Management | 5 |
| | 1.3 Various soil and water conservation projects | 6 |
| | 1.4 Present status of soil and water conservation in India | 7 |
| | 1.5 Sustainable Agricultural Development | 10 |
| 2. | **People's participation in soil and water conservation** | **11-20** |
| | 2.1 The origin of participation | 11 |
| | 2.2 Concept of people's participation | 12 |
| | 2.3 Benefits of people's participation | 16 |
| | 2.4 Types of people's participation | 16 |
| | 2.5 People's participation in progamme stages | 18 |
| 3. | **People's participation in soil and water conservation for sustainable agricultural production in the Antisar watershed of Gujarat - a case study** | **21-142** |
| | 3.1 Introduction | 21 |
| | 3.2 Significance of the study | 22 |
| | 3.3 Justification of the sample | 22 |
| | 3.4 Justification of the variables | 23 |
| | 3.5 Objectives of the study | 28 |
| | 3.6 Methodology | 34 |
| | 3.7 Findings | 53 |

| Sr. No. | CHAPTERS | Page No. |
|---|---|---|
| 4. | **Participatory approach based on discussion of findings** | **143-174** |
| | 4.1 Profile of the respondents | 143 |
| | 4.2 Risk preference of farmers towards SWC technologies | 145 |
| | 4.3 Knowledge levels of respondents regarding SWC technologies | 146 |
| | 4.4 Attitude of farmers towards SWC programme | 147 |
| | 4.5 Adoption of SWC technologies | 149 |
| | 4.6 People's participation in SWC programme | 150 |
| | 4.7 Relationship between the overall participation and selected variables | 152 |
| | 4.8 Relationship between the participation in planning and variables | 157 |
| | 4.9 Relationship between the participation in implementation and variables | 162 |
| | 4.10 Relationship between the participation in maintenance and variables | 167 |
| | 4.11 Relationship between the people's participation in SWC programme and the variable gender | 172 |
| | 4.12 Constraints faced by respondents | 172 |
| | 4.13 Criteria for participatory approach in watershed management | 173 |
| 5 | **Cited literature** | **175-176** |
| 6 | **Bibliography** | **177-178** |
| 7 | **Appendix** | **179-190** |
| 8 | **Index** | **191-192** |

******

# PREFACE

People's participation is imperative in soil and water conservation programme through watershed approach. It is a collective and cooperative effort by the local people for sharing common benefits. Participation of local people at the time of preparing a watershed development programme is very much needed to take decisions because the programme should be according to the basic needs of local people. The programme should meet the basic needs of the majority of the local people like supply of drinking water, fodder for cattle and fuel for kitchen. The local people are the ultimate beneficiary of any programme. Therefore, the programme should be for the people, by the people and of the people.

The watershed development programmes are made for local people, hence the local people should take interest and participate in implementation of programme by contributing labour and money in construction of soil and water conservation structures on their field and common land. Participation in maintenance is also required because without protection and care by the local people the programme will not be successful. The involvement of local people in evaluation of programme is also necessary, so that it may provide points to be considered for improvement in future programme planning.

Thus, it was felt to conduct a research study and write the book on the people's participation in soil and water conservation programme for sustainable agricultural production through watershed approach.

It is my privilege and great pleasure to express my deepest sense of gratitude and sincere thanks to Dr. Uma Joshi, Head, Department of Home Science Extension and Communication, Faculty of Home Science, The Maharaja Sayajirao University of Baroda for her learned counsel, guidance, encouraging attitude, abundant interest and continuous inspiration for the present study and writing the book.

My most sincere and very special thanks is also due to Dr. J.S. Samra, Deputy Director General (Natural Resources Management), Indian Council of Agricultural Research, New Delhi, for constant guidance and sanctioning my study leave for taking up the research study. I also express my gratitude to Dr. V. N. Sharda, Director, Central Soil and Water Conservation Research and Training Institute, Dehradun for his constant guidance in research study and help in writing the book.

I express my gratitude and thanks to Dr. K. F. Patel, Associate Director of Extension Education (Zone), Gujarat Agricultural University, Anand, for his sincere guidance and help in writing the book based on my research study on people's participation.

I express my sincere thanks to Prof. Anupama Shah, Ex-Dean and Prof. Kalpana Parlikar, Ex-Head, Department of Home Science Extension and Communication, Faculty of Home Science, The Maharaja Sayajirao University of Baroda for their valuable suggestions and advice provided during research study and writing the book.

I also acknowledge the cooperation extended to me by the Scientists of the Central Soil and Water Conservation Research and Training Institute (CSWCRTI), Research Centre, Vasad.

My thanks are also extended to Ms. D.S. Macwan, Personal Assistant, CSWCRTI, Research Centre, Vasad, for patiently typing the manuscript.

Lastly but not least, I express my gratitude to my parents and special thanks to my wife Mrs. Anita Bagdi for their moral support and help provided during the research study and in writing the book.

**G.L. BAGDI**

# CHAPTER 1

# SOIL AND WATER CONSERVATION THROUGH WATERSHED APPROACH

## 1.1 WATERSHED

Watershed is an area in which rain water flows from highest point to lowest point and drains out through a natural stream outlet. A watershed is a catchment area, which drains water and other runoff materials to a common outlet through a natural drainage system. It is also known as drainage basin and catchment. The size of a watershed can vary from a small field of a farmer to a large river basin. A watershed is suggested to be the most scientific unit for efficient and sustainable management of natural resources i.e. land and water. In a watershed approach, a suitable and manageable size of watershed is selected for making maximum output from the available and rational use of limited resources within the watershed. Several preliminary exercises are carried out through the watershed development agency to generate basic information about the watershed and watershed inhabitants. The important aspects on which the watershed information collected are socio-economic status of farmers, vegetation, land use survey, and hydrological information. Participatory Rural Appraisal (PRA) technique is used to interact with the local farmers to know about watershed situation and resources. PRA technique is recently developed and used to assess the socio-economic status of watershed, agricultural practices adopted by farmers for soil and water conservation and the problems prevailing in watershed and suggestion from the farmers for development of a watershed. PRA technique is used before actual implementation of soil and water conservation programme for watershed development. It is useful in helping people to help themselves by analyzing their living conditions. Based on the PRA information, suitable measures of improved soil and water conservation technologies, crop development, afforestation, pasture development and horticulture development are taken in the watershed management. Watershed management is the rational and proper use of natural resources that are land and water for sustainable agricultural production.

Swaminathan (1998) said rainfed agriculture to be productive, should be based on a watershed as the unit of development. Watershed is not technology but a concept, which integrates conservation, management and budgeting of rainwater through simple but discrete hydrological units. Simultaneously, a watershed supports a holistic framework which means a combined application of technologies on soil and water conservation with improved crop varieties, farming systems and agronomic management, taking into account both arable and non-farm land.

The idea of integrated treatment of all lands on a watershed was adopted and implemented by Damodar Valley Corporation as early as in 1949. The watershed is a continuous area whose runoff water drains to a common point, so it facilitates water harvesting and moisture concentration. Integrated watershed management focuses on combining improved farming practices with soil and water conservation and appropriate land use. Watershed approach refers to both the types of farming i.e. irrigated and rainfed (dry land) and widely differs in their approach but the concept remains more or less the same. It also includes both arable and non-arable land and, therefore, needs equal emphasis in terms of improvement for maintaining ecological balance and sustainable development. Also, the concept of integrated treatment of all lands on a watershed basis to improve the moisture retention capacity of soil and to minimize the soil erosions by effectively checking the flow of excess runoff rain water is important specially in dryland/rainfed areas. The specific objectives of the watershed programme include promotion of soil and water conservation, optimal use of land and water resources (Singh, 1993).

According to Singh (1990) watershed constitutes a basic unit of development of rainfed areas. It is a holistic approach encompassing a process of economic planning to obviate the twin problems of rainfed agriculture-low productivity and instability through an integrated approach. Unlike the earlier isolated efforts through soil conservation or crop production or use of any other agro-technique in a disjointed manner, the watershed approach aims at optimizing the use of land, water and vegetation in an area in an integrated way and thus help alleviate drought, moderate floods, prevent soil erosion, improve water availability, increase fuel, fodder and agricultural production on a sustained basis.

In physical terms, a watershed refers to the area lying above a given drainage point. In functional terms, the watershed programme tends to become synonymous with the area development; in the present context, the central theme begins the improvement of dry lands.

The main thrust of watershed development is to rationalize conservation and utilization of natural resources and other inputs to optimize productivity, stability and prosperity of the area. The main components which should be integrated in watershed development programmes are as follows:

    i)    Conservation, management and development of soil resources,

    ii)   Conservation, management and development of water resources,

    iii)  Efficient crop management and improved cropping intensity, and

    iv)  Alternate land use systems according to land capability.

## 1.2 WHY WATERSHED MANAGEMENT ?

Singh et al. (1990) stated that by and large, most of the arid and semi-arid regions have been overlooked by the development planners and researchers. It is only in recent years; little attention has been paid about the problems of these areas. These regions have concentrations of eroded and degraded natural resources. Loss of vegetative cover followed by soil degradation through various forms of erosion has resulted in lands which are thirsty in terms of water as well as hungry in terms of soil nutrients. All these regions have predominantly livestock-centred farming systems; less biomass for animals not only reduces animal productivity but subsequent intense grazing pressures on already eroded lands further exacerbate the problem and deteriorate the ecological balance. Growing population pressure, higher demand for food and fodder coupled with impact of rapidly changing socio-economic conditions has added fuel to the fire.

The piecemeal approaches such as contour bunding or terracing on individual holdings or a group of farms only marginally benefit as they are done ignoring to what happens to other areas, which are influencing the hydrologic characteristics. Such sporadic actions generally fail to attract farmers, as they do not yield benefits commensurating with the efforts and investments made. Thus, for maximizing the advantages, all developmental activities should be undertaken in a comprehensive way on watershed basis. The main principles of watershed management are:

i) Utilizing the land according to its capability.
ii) Putting adequate vegetal cover on the soil during the rainy season.
iii) Conserving as much rain water as possible at the place where it falls.
iv) Draining out excess water with a safe velocity and diverting it to storage ponds and store it for future use.
v) Avoiding gully formation and putting checks at suitable intervals to control soil erosion and recharge ground water.
vi) Maximizing productivity per unit area, per unit time and per unit of water.
vii) Increasing cropping intensity and land equivalent ratio through intercropping and sequence cropping.
viii) Safe utilization of marginal lands through alternate land use systems.
ix) Ensuring sustainability of the Eco-systems befitting the man-animal-plant-land water complex in the watershed.
x) Maximizing the combined income from the inter-related and dynamic crop livestock-tree-labour complex over years.
xi) Stabilizing total income and cut down risks during aberrant weather situations.
xii) Improving infrastructure facilities with regard to storage, transportation and marketing.

## 1.3 VARIOUS SOIL AND WATER CONSERVATION PROJECTS

Watershed Development Projects have been taken up under different programmes launched by the Government of India. The Drought Prone Area Programme (DPAP) and the Desert Development Programme (DDP) adopted the watershed approach in 1987. The Integrated Wasteland Development Projects Scheme (IWDP) taken up by the National Wasteland Development Board in 1989 also aimed at developing wastelands on a watershed basis. This programme has now been brought under the administrative jurisdiction of the Department of Wastelands Development in the Ministry of Rural Development. The fourth major programme based on the watershed concept is the National Watershed Development Programme in Rainfed Areas (NWDPRA) under the Ministry of Agriculture (Anonymous, 1994).

So far, these programmes have laid down their own separate guidelines, norms, funding patterns and technical components based on their respective and specific aims. While the Desert Development Programme focussed on reforestation to arrest the growth of hot and cold deserts, the Drought Prone Areas Programme concentrated on non-arable lands and drainage lines for *in-situ* soil and moisture conservation, agro-forestry, pasture development, horticulture and alternate land uses. The Integrated Wasteland Development projects, on the other hand, made silvi pasture, soil and moisture conservation on wastelands under government or community or private control as their predominant activity. The NWDPRA combines the features of all these three programmes with the additional dimension of improving arable lands through better crop management technologies.

### National Watershed Development Programme for Rainfed Agriculture (NWDPRA): A scheme of Government of India

National Watershed Development Programme for Rainfed Agricultural (NWDPRA) was initiated during 1986-87 and is being looked after by the Crops Division of the Department of Agricultural and Cooperation. Development of the rainfed dry land areas has been given a very high priority during the $7^{th}$ as well as for $8^{th}$ Plan; and it forms item 2 of the 20 Point Programme – 1986 of the Govt. of India. The main objectives of the NWDPRA are to conserve and upgrade both crop lands and cultivable wastelands on watershed basis to stabilize and increase crop yields from rainfed farming, to augment the fruit, fodder and fuel resources through appropriate alternate land use systems, and to develop and disseminate technologies for proper soil and moisture conservation required under different conditions. The priority objective, however, is stabilization of agricultural production in rainfed areas which constitute nearly 68% of the total area of the country comprising 33% in the low rainfall region (<750 mm) and 35% under medium rainfall region (750-1175 mm). The NWDPRA is being implemented in the unirrigated arable lands mostly falling in the rainfall range of 500 to 1125 mm.

The districts having more than 30% area under irrigation are generally excluded from this programme (Singh, 1990).

**The major components of the programme are as follows:**
   i) Land and moisture management including scientifically tuned cropping system, dryland horticulture, fodder production and farm forestry.
   ii) Contingency seed and planting material stocking.
   iii) Training, seminars study tours for staff and farmers within the state/region/national level.
   iv) Adaptive research trials on different crops in small and marginal farmers' fields.
   v) Procurement, fabrication and supply of survey equipment and prototype implements.
   v) Preparation of field manuals and publicity materials.

## 1.4 PRESENT STATUS OF SOIL AND WATER CONSERVATION IN INDIA

As a consequence of increasing pressure on land, the natural balance between the soil forming and soil conserving processes has been affected leading to serious problems of soil erosion. According to a rough estimate, out of the total geographical area of 329 m ha of our country, about 173 million hectare is subjected to varying degrees and forms of soil erosion. This includes about 80 m ha of agricultural land, 20 m ha of degraded forest land, 13 m ha of permanent pastures and grazing lands, 29 m ha of barren and uncultivable land, etc. About 3.67 m ha are reported to be under ravines. Denudation of forest in various watersheds has resulted in floods and torrents. There are also the problems of landslides and silting of reservoirs and rivers. The erosion rates in some of the areas are indeed alarming. About 5334 million tonnes of soil (16.35 t/ha/year) is being eroded annually. About 29% of eroded material is permanently lost into sea. About 5.37 to 8.40 million tonnes of soil nutrients are lost through water erosion (Anonymous, 1998).

India was among first few countries to have taken timely cognizance of the enormity of the problem. Large scale soil and water conservation activity began in 1950's with the establishment of a chain of Soil Conservation Research, Demonstration and Training Centres by the Govt of India in different problem areas, located at Dehradun, Kota, Bellary, Ootacamund, Vasad, Agra and Chandigarh. Besides these centres, a centre was also established at Ibrahimpatnam (Hyderabad) on 12.10.1962, which later became headquarters of All India Crop Research Project (AICRP) for dryland agriculture. Now, it is known as Central Research Institute for Dryland Agriculture (CRIDA) at Hyderabad.

These centres were transferred to the Indian Council of Agricultural Research (ICAR), New Delhi, on 1st October, 1967. The ICAR combined these Research Centres and established on 1st April, 1974, the Central Soil and Water Conservation Research and Training Institute (CSWCRTI) with the headquarters at Dehradun. A new Research Centre at Datia (M.P.) was established on 18.9.1986 to tackle the soil and water conservation problems of Bundelkhand region in Uttar Pradesh and Madhya Pradesh. Another new Research Centre at Koraput (Orissa) was established on 31.1.1992 to tackle the problem of shifting cultivation in the lateritic soils of Eastern Ghats and Kondhan Hills.

Research and development activities of the Central Soil and Water Conservation Research and Training Institute, Dehradun and centres focussed on evolving strategies of soil and water conservation on watershed basis, tackling special problems such as ravines, landslides, minespoils and torrents demonstration of technology for popularization and imparting training. Reclamation technologies of torrent gullies, landslides, mine spoils, gravelly/ boulders soils, sloping lands, watershed restoration, runoff harvesting alternate land uses, diversification, bio-diversity (ecological successions), bio-remediation, management common property resources and community participation were amply demonstrated with fairly good degrees of successes.

Experimental watersheds were set up in 1956 with monitoring devices for generating watersheds-based protection and production technologies. From 1974 onward, the Institute pioneered in operationalizing the watershed concepts through four famous Operational Research Projects at Sukhomajri (Haryana State). Nada (Chandigarh), Fakot (Tehri-Garhwal in UP), G.R. Halli (Chitradurga, Karnataka state). With the experience gained from the watershed, the ICAR launched 47 model watershed programmes in sixteen states in collaboration with State Agricultural Universities and State Departments. Encouraged with the success of the model watersheds, the Ministry of Agriculture and Rural Development conceived of a massive development programme through 10,000 watersheds for soil and water conservation and sustainable development.

Paroda (2000) stated that India with an area of 329 million hectares is the $7^{th}$ largest country in the world. And its share in land resources is only 2 per cent, but it sustains 18 per cent and 15 per cent of the global human and livestock population. The pressure on land is constantly on increase and our human population has already crossed 1 billion mark. As per the estimates of the National Bureau of Soil Survey and Land Use Planning (1994), about 57 per cent of the total geographical area of the country is suffering from various forms of degradation – water erosion, wind erosion, chemical and physical deterioration, besides, degradation on account of mining, quarrying, landslides, and urbanization, there are alarming trends in shift of prime agricultural land to non-agricultural uses.

India has a net sown area of 142.5 million hectares, which is next only to the USA and more than that of China. Somehow, this has remained static since the beginning of the 90's. The per capita availability of agricultural land being 0.53 ha in 1950 has decreased to 0.14 ha at present, and is likely to decline further to 0.08 ha by 2020. This implies that there is practically no scope for horizontal expansion of agriculture. Thus, in future we will have to produce more food from less and less of land and in an environmentally sustainable manner.

The land falling in marginal to sub-marginal class, which is better suited for pastures, forests and range lands have also been brought under cultivation of crop, a proposition that is neither economically viable nor environmentally sustainable. Although the net irrigated area has increased from 22.56 million hectares in 1950-51 to 55.14 million ha, which is the highest in the world, the cropping intensity has increased marginally from 111 per cent to 132.7 per cent in the corresponding period. Therefore, future production increases must come through vertical expansion, mainly through improved cultivars, judicious input use and increasing cropping intensity by 15-20 per cent with emphasis on legumes.

Our soils are more hungry now than ever before, and they are low in organic matter content due to continuous cultivation and siphoning of soil nutrients. Current status indicates that the N deficiency is universal and nearly 49, 20 and 47 per cent soils are deficient in P, K and Zn, respectively. Similarly, Fe, Mn and B deficiencies have also surfaced in some pockets. In addition, more than 5.3 billion tonnes of top soil is lost every year due to erosion resulting in a net loss of around 8 million tonnes of plant nutrients and 3 million tonnes of foodgrains.

The green revolution technologies are the cornerstone of our agricultural growth, which often relied on intensive use of inputs, especially water and inorganic fertilizers. Though we had witnessed quantum jumps in foodgrains production, the continuous and sometimes indiscriminate use of inputs had also adversely affected the health of our soil. Hence, a balanced and integrated water and nutrient management approach has to be put into place to ensure sustainability of our production systems.

The best means of improving sustainability of farming systems is to prevent any further degradation of land resources and adopting alternate agricultural practices/technologies related to soil conservation, crop rotation, conservation tillage, integrated nutrient management with improved input-use efficiencies etc.

Obviously, therefore, this is a strong case to go for scientific land-use planning commensurate with land capability class and its carrying capacity. In recognition of this, the ICAR is strengthening research on "Land Use Planning for the Resource Sustainability" under the National Agricultural Technology Project (NATP) in a Mission-Mode approach.

We must strive for safeguarding our natural resources for posterity since they rightly belong to future generations and we must hand these over to them at least in a better state than what we inherited from our ancestors. Therefore, scientific land-use planning needs to be pursued.

## 1.5 SUSTAINABLE AGRICULTURAL DEVELOPMENT

The 25$^{th}$ FAO Conference, November, 1989, adopted the following definition of sustainable development: Sustainable development is the management and conservation of the natural resource base, and the orientation of technological and institutional change in such a manner as to ensure the attainment and continued satisfaction of human needs for present and future generations. Such sustainable development (in the agriculture, forestry and fisheries sectors) conserves land, water, plant and animal genetic resources, and is environmentally non-degrading, technically appropriate, economically viable and socially acceptable (FAO, 1989).

The sustainable agriculture is that a cultivation practice, which over a long period of time enhances soil fertility, provides fuel, fodder and food to farmers. Sustainable agriculture should be environmentally suitable, economically viable and socially acceptable for upliftment of farmers and rural village society as a whole.

## CHAPTER 2

# PEOPLE'S PARTICIPATION IN SOIL AND WATER CONSERVATION

## 2.1 THE ORIGIN OF PARTICIPATION

Santhanam (1982) stated that although the concept of participation gained importance in recent times, its origin can be traced to Aristotle, the Greek Scholar. Aristotle was of the opinion that participating in the affairs of the state as a citizen was essential to the development and fulfilment of the human personality. He felt that exclusion from politics indicated that one did not develop fully the faculty of reason, a sense of responsibility for other's welfare and a disposal towards prudent and balanced judgement. At societal level, Aristotle found clear relationship between the extent of participation and the creation of good life. According to him, the best state was one where there was broad participation with no class dominating others. Aristotle's analysis showed some relationship between the participation and development. He mentioned that some conditions of development at the societal level were necessary for productive participation yet such participation was needed for development at the individual level. The relationship is complex because participation has economic, social and political dimensions.

In international development scenario, the concept of people's participation emerged through disenchantment with the growth-oriented, top-down dominant development paradigm. As assumptions underlying this dominant paradigm (such as that the benefits accruing from development programmes will trickle down from the upper strata of the society to the lower strata) failed to come true the concept of 'alternative development' also referred to as 'counter development', emerged in the 1970s. This thesis strongly advocated community participation as a pre-requisite for equitable development.

People's participation is, however, not a new idea in India. In fact, it emerged long ago in the vision and actions of Tagore and Gandhi. Rural masses as development actors were the central feature of their rural reconstruction programme. But the concept in the form we know it today is essentially a post-Independence phenomenon. Right since the beginning of planned development, people's participation was considered instrumental in realizing the goals of planning. The first Five Year Plan stated that, 'No plan can have any chance of success unless the millions of small farmers in the country accept its objectives, share in its making, regard it as their own and are prepared to make sacrifices necessary for implementing it. Therefore, the nationwide Community Development Programme (CDP) launched to bring about socio-economic and cultural transformation of the countryside, made professions for popular participation in planning and implementation of development programmes though Gram Panchayat, Block Advisory Committees and District Boards.

It was soon realized, however, that the CDP, instead of being people's programme with government's support, was becoming more and more government's programme with varying degree of people's participation. People's participation was substituted by bureaucratic mobilization directed toward achieving set goals of development.

Poor performance of CDP prompted the policy makers to appoint a Study Team under the Chairmanship of Shri Balvantrai Mehta in 1957 to examine and assess the functioning of the programme. The Study Team remarked that in order to be self-sustaining and self-generating, development has to go hand-in-hand with participation. If found the ability to invoke popular participation as one of the least successful aspects of CDP. It therefore recommended a devolution of power and a decentralization of machinery controlled and directed by popular representatives of the local area.

Based on these recommendations, people's participation was institutionalized with the launch of Panchayati Raj System in India on 2$^{nd}$ October, 1959. Since then the Panchayati Raj System has been experimented within different states with all kinds of variations in its structure, implementation resource allocation, staffing pattern and the degree of autonomy allowed to different units.

## 2.2 CONCEPT OF PEOPLE'S PARTICIPATION

People's participation can be defined as "concerted efforts by a group of local participants for achieving common goals and sharing benefits". The other scientists also defined people's participation as given below :

Peabody (1965) opined that participation would consist of a specific action for a limited purpose.

Karl Deutsch (1969) considered participation as a technique for setting goals, choosing priorities and deciding on the kind of resources to commit to achieve goal attainment.

United Nations Social Development Division (1973) defined participation "as a process of activities comprising people's involvement in decision making, contributing to the development efforts shared equitably in the benefits derived therefrom".

In his paper on the psychological aspects of community development, Muthayya (1973) points out that the idea of participation emphasizes a process of social action in which the people of the community organize themselves for identifying their common needs and problems, plan a course of action with maximum reliance upon community resources and supplement the resources when necessary, with service and material from governmental and non-governmental agencies outside the community. He further states that participation in the real sense should involve people in any programme based on mutual respect. It involves a capacity to identify oneself with others in the community without being conscious of any socio-economic barriers.

An overall review of the literature available on "participation" throws light on its varied aspects. If these aspects are classified into a specific pattern, the classification can be done as "person", "process" and "product". Although there is no consensus on the usage of the term participation, many definitions have emphasized mostly the "process" of participation starting from the 'decision-making' or 'setting up of goals', etc. The foregoing review indicates invariably the 'social change' as a "product", not adequately recognizing the importance of the 'person' which consists of the 'human factors' in participation and in bringing about the social change. Such human factors on which the processes of participation depends should also be given due importance lest effective participation may not be assured for achieving the set goal. The 'participation' or 'involvement' as same would prefer it, will be effective only when it is strongly and adequately reinforced by the awareness of the existing social situation, attitude towards it, felt-need or motivation to achieve the goal, viz. social change.

Any programme that aims at bringing about social change by an active participation of people themselves, should be prepared considering the human factors involved therein and also which will be further facilitated by future reinforcement. Moreover, such participation will be enhanced by committed citizens when there will be no class consciousness or barriers in achieving the goals. This was well noted by Aristotle in defining a best state as the one where as broad participation occurs with no class dominating the others. Modernizing it, Muthayya (1973) makes participation as an involvement on the part of the individual without any socio-economic barriers to achieve the goal in a group situation. This aspect is considered here since importance is given to the individual, the socio-cultural and economic status as these have more impact on an individual and in shaping his behavioural pattern. Considering all those phenomena, one may well conceptualize 'participation' as "commitment on the part of the individual towards all forms of action through which he can 'take part' or 'play a role' in the operation without being conscious of any socio-economic barriers to achieve certain common goals in a group situation". This involvement or commitment would be influenced only if he is effectively appraised about the situation so as to enable him to form an attitude based on his own perception of the situation with this concept of participation in mind the present investigation is aimed to study some of the basic components of behavioural aspects which facilitate the effective participation.

Moulik (1978) is of the opinion that "participation in development process implies stimulating individuals to take the initiative and mobilizing people to work for overall societal development".

In spite of its importance, in most of the present rural development strategies, the element of people's participation is left a shade nebulous. There is confusion and vagueness regarding the understanding of the concept. According to Jagannadhan (1979), "involvement" may be a more appropriate term and a more acceptable concept than "participation". He elaborates stating that while participation implies sharing, involvement connotes a "sense of belongingness".

Sir Desmond Heap is also of the opinion that participation and involvement should be differentiated. He defines citizen participation as "the active participation in decision-making process" and citizen involvement as "awareness of policies through consultations". These writers interpret participation as meaning "sharing in decision-making" which, it presupposes knowledge, information, competence, acceptability, and a host of other qualities and capabilities which are generally rare among the people.

Some consider that financial assistance rendered under any programme by an individual or a group is a mode of participation. Some others felt that taking part in an activity by giving one's own labour, i.e. Shramdan is also participation; still others think that a person who can contribute neither financially nor by labour but can guide the group/activity by mobilizing resources is also said to be participating in the programme; in politics, casting vote is said to be participation and in the organizational set-up, membership and attending meetings actively or passively is taken as participation.

As there seems to be an overlapping in the meaning of the terms participation and involvement an attempt is made here to put forth the available definitions and/or descriptions of participation and evolve a suitable meaning to the concept for the purpose of the study.

Sharma (1979) viewed participation in two aspects: in the broadest sense, the term participation is used to refer to all those actions taken by people to take part in the process of social change. Participation is not regarded as having been committed to any social goals but is regarded as a technique of setting goals, choosing priorities and deciding to generate the resources to the achievement of the goal. In a restricted sense participation consists in a specific action by which the people participate for achievement of a limited goal. In this case, the citizen does not confine himself to expressing an opinion on specific measures but directly participates in the achievement of the objectives.

Cohen and Uphoff (1980) describe participation as "people's involvement in decision-making process about what would be done and how; their involvement in implementing programmes and decisions by contributing various resources or cooperate in specific organizations or activities, their sharing in the benefits of development programmes and/or their involvement in efforts to evaluate such programmes. Taken together, these four kinds of involvement appear to encompass most of what would generally be referred to as participation in development activities".

Further, they regard participation as "generally denoting the involvement of a significant number of persons in situations or actions which enhance their well-being, e.g. their income, security or self-esteem".

Hunter (1980) describes participation as that which "implies that farmers themselves have a major role say in the choice of the innovative programme, in deciding on the methods to be used and in organizing their own contribution of labour and management".

Verhagen (1980) is of the opinion that "participation is generally presented as the active involvement of target groups in the planning, implementation and control programmes and projects and not merely their passive acquiescence in performing predetermined tasks, not merely their exploitation in order to reduce the labour cost. Participation, it is argued, guarantees that the beneficiaries' own interests are taken into account. This enhances the likelihood that programmes and projects will prove effective in meeting felt development needs and that participants share equitably in all benefits".

According to Yadav (1980) people's participation means "involvement of the people in the development process voluntarily and willingly. Such participation cannot be coerced". He states that people's involvement has to be understood in terms of participation in decision-making, implementation of development programmes, monitoring and evaluation of such programmes and in sharing the benefits of development.

According to Banki (1981), "People's participation is a dynamic group process in which all members of a group contribute to the attainment of group objectives, share the benefits from group activities, exchange information and experience of common interest, and follow the rules, regulations and other decisions made by the group".

Mishra (1984) stated that in broadly speaking participation is understood as the "involvement of a significant number of persons in situations or actions, which enhance their well-being".

Jose (1994) has been defined participation as the process of taking part, having said, or being able to influence the design, implementation or the outcome of a development project.

Mishra (1994) stated that in practice, the term participation has three connotations. Participation means cooperating, taking part in something the more presence, even silent present of an individual or representative of an organization at different levels. Participation can be direct or indirect, active or passive. It can occur at any level from lower rung to higher hone from village level to the national level. It is one of the important techniques to achieve the desired goal.

## 2.3 BENEFITS OF PEOPLE'S PARTICIPATION

The major benefits flowing from the participation of the people in development are: in the planning and programming stages and throughout the implementation of development programmes, rural people can provide valuable social-cultural, ecological, economic and technical indigenous knowledge ensuring consistency between objectives of development and community values and preferences; people can mobilize local resources in the form of cash, labour, materials, managerial talent and political support which are critical to programme success; Programmes involving people are more likely to sustain after outside financial and technical support is withdrawn; Participation by the poorer elements of the society may prevent the "hijacking" of programme benefits by wealthier members of the community; People accept more readily the programmes in which they or their recognized leaders have been involved. They feel that it is their programme; Involvement of local people in decision making generates commitment for implementation of the programme; it enhances people's ability to take responsibility and show competence in solving their own problems (Tyagi, 1998).

## 2.4 TYPES OF PEOPLE'S PARTICIPATION

The types or forms of people's participation were suggested by different scientists in various ways but the most important classifications which are suitable to watershed development are suggested as below :

According to the author the types or forms of people's participation in soil and water conservation programmes can be divided into the following:

i) **Participation as material :**

The local people having good socio-economic status and farm resources can participate more by providing help of their materials, equipments, machines and implements during construction of different soil and water conservation (SWC) structures in watershed development area.

ii) **Participation as money :**

Farmers can also contribute money in the form of participation in construction of different SWC structures on their own land or on community land. So that the farmers will take care and protect the structures, because their money is involved in construction of soil and water conservation structures.

### iii) Participation as labour :

Poor farmers, who are unable to participate in the form of money, they can participate by contributing their labour work in construction of SWC structures on their own land as well as on community/Panchayat land also.

### iv) Participation as guidance :

The old and experienced local farmers of the village can also participate in the planning and designing of soil and water conservation programmes by suggesting their ideas and past experiences. The suggestions of experienced people's in the form of feedback is good to be included in the planning of SWC programme, that will provide more benefits to the local participants from the SWC programme. Local farmers can also provide their local techniques to carry out different SWC works in rural development programme.

According to Jose (1994) the people's participation is also divided into four types:

### (i) Participation as contribution :

Participation as contribution implies voluntary or other forms of contributions by beneficiaries to predetermined programmes and projects. The level of participation in management tends to be low. Beneficiary involvement in the programme implementation is limited to same contribution or to a limited extend of resource mobilization. The low involvement mainly arises from the lack of community capacity. Community capacity refers to the skill level within the beneficiaries to structure, analyze, generate and evaluate solutions to the problems facing the community.

### (ii) Participation as organization :

The next higher level of participation involves changing/reorienting the administrative environment. This form of participation will take place when the beneficiaries are co-opted into the administering agency (beneficiary representatives on the board of the local authority). The advantage of such participation at its higher levels is that it lets the beneficiaries determine the nature and structure of the organization. This also affords the beneficiaries enhanced roles in the planning, selection and implementation stages of the programme. The process is essentially a bureaucratic re-orientation process. The administering authority now has to give up some of the powers of control enjoyed by it in the past. The lowest level examples of this are decentralization of the central administering agency and the co-option of beneficiary representatives, which result in facilitating the creation of beneficiary organizations.

### (iii) Participation as partnership :

Emphasis in this mode is on the development of skills and abilities that enable beneficiaries to manage their resource better (i.e. in sustainable and productive manner), and have a say in or negotiate with existing delivery systems (voice). At a higher level this occurs when the beneficiaries get together to form their own organizations (with the help of the development administration) such as farmers' cooperatives, irrigation committees etc.

Participation as partnership operates on the philosophy that given sufficient support and training people are capable of managing their own affairs. In recent times this has been the attitude of most developmental agencies to development in the rural sector. The beneficiaries have a substantial say in the selection and the administration of the developmental activity. Logically, it means that at the highest levels of participation in this mode the beneficiaries may select or reject a programme based on the criteria they may have set for themselves.

Two points need to be noted with regard to this mode. One, the development administrations role, in most cases, is limited to an advisory one and one of securing the necessary inputs and liaison with the external official machinery. Two, the development agency may withdraw at a later stage without crippling the programme.

### (iv) Participation as empowering :

Participation as empowerment is the process of enabling the beneficiaries to decide upon and to take actions, which they perceive as essential to their development. This is essentially a political process and the beneficiaries in this case would enjoy the maximum voice possible in any form of participation. Development of power to local administrative authorities is an example of this mode of management. Voluntary organizations very often resort to this process of participate management.

## 2.5 PEOPLE'S PARTICIPATION IN PROGRAMME STAGES

People's participation in natural resources conservation programme through watershed management is utmost important at different stages viz.; i) programme planning, ii) programme implementation, iii) programme maintenance and iv) programme evaluation. It is a collective and cooperative effort by the local people for sharing common benefits.

### i) People's participation in programme planning :

People's participation at the time of preparing a watershed development programme is very much needed to take decisions because the programme should be according to the basic needs of local people. The programme should meet the basic needs of the majority of the local people like supply of drinking water, fodder for cattle and fuel for kitchen. The local people are the ultimate beneficiary of any programme. Therefore, the programme should be for the people, by the people and of the people.

### ii) People's participation in programme implementation :

The watershed development programmes are made for local people, hence the local people should take interest and participate in implementation of programme by contributing labour and money in construction of soil and water conservation structures on their field and common land/Panchayat land.

### iii) People's participation in programme maintenance :

Participation in maintenance is required because without protection and care of soil and water conservation structures on their land as well as on community land by the local people the programme will not be successful. The local people should maintain and repair the damaged and breached structures by their own money and labour contribution.

### iv) People's participation in programme evaluation :

The involvement of local people in evaluation of soil and water conservation programme is also necessary, so that it may provide points to be considered for improvement in future programme planning; implementation and maintenance stages.

Therefore, the concept of soil and water conservation through watershed area basis was taken to reduce the soil degradation. The natural resources such as soil and water should be managed properly for sustainable agricultural production. There should be rational use of natural resources that are soil and water for sustainable agricultural production through the concept of watershed. The watershed is not a technology of soil and water conservation. Whereas, watershed is a concept according to that the soil and water conservation technologies should be adopted according to the contour lines of a catchment area from highest to lowest point. According to the participatory approach, the soil and water conservation programmes for watershed development are developed by the rural farmers, for the rural farmers and of the rural farmers. The participation of local rural farmers is imperative for implementation and maintenance of Soil and Water Conservation programmes. Hence, a need was felt to conduct a research study to know whether, the rural farmers actively participate in soil and water conservation programme on watershed basis during planning, implementation, maintenance stages or not at all concerned with natural resources conservation.

Therefore, a research study was framed to assess the extent of people's participation in Soil and Water Conservation for sustainable agricultural production in watershed as presented in detail in the succeeding Chapter 3. The study was also focussing to assess the knowledge level of farmer's regarding soil and water conservation practices. The attitude of farmers towards Soil and Water Conservation technologies and extent of adoption of SWC technologies were also be studied. It is also emphasized to analyze the different problems faced by the farmers and farm women during Soil and Water Conservation programme.

# CHAPTER 3

# PEOPLE'S PARTICIPATION IN SOIL AND WATER CONSERVATION FOR SUSTAINABLE AGRICULTURAL PRODUCTION IN THE ANTISAR WATERSHED OF GUJARAT– A CASE STUDY

## 3.1 INTRODUCTION

Land degradation is a continuous process caused by soil erosion due to rain water and wind. According to the present scenario, a considerable amount of soil i.e. about 5334 million tonnes is eroded every year. The land degradation today threatens the livelihoods of rural poor farmers. The agricultural production is going to be decreased year after year under the erosion affected lands and poor farmers become poorer. The situation is more dangerous in arid areas, where only rainfed crops are cultivated. The poor farmers are unable to grow crops even as much as needed to feed their own family members throughout the year. Particularly, in Gujarat State a very extensive degradation of land has occurred along the banks of the rivers; Banas, Sabarmati, Vatrak, Mahi, Tapi and Naramda. This continuous extensive degradation of soil has developed big gullies on the land, which is known as ravines and also popularly known as "Kotar" in Gujarati.

It seems from the present situation of the country that the environment, problem has increased due to deforestation in rural areas. The rural people cut down the forests tremendously for their own consumption. By cutting down the forests the environmental imbalance is created and the water level of the area also decreases. This leads to the agricultural land converted in barren land due to lack of water and environmental hazards. Therefore, to increase the agricultural production the soil and water conservation is at most required. Therefore, the local people in the rural areas should participate in conserving the natural resources such as soil and water conservation for reconverting the barren land into the agricultural land. Soil and water are the natural resources essential for survival of people on earth. People should realize the importance of conserving the soil and water. There should be judicial utilization of soil and water for sustainable agricultural production. This requires participation of people at all levels of soil and water conservation programme.

This study will help to find out factors responsible for people's participation in soil and water conservation programme. It will also analyze the constraints faced by the rural farmers during soil and water conservation programme and draw out the suggestions to overcome these constraints by adopting a participatory approach.

Hence, it is very much important to measure and assess the level of people's participation in soil and water conservation programmes.

## 3.2 SIGNIFICANCE OF THE STUDY

Improved soil and water conservation technologies are very essential for conserving the natural resources. The concept of watershed management is in vogue for soil and water conservation for sustainable agricultural production in rural areas. Keeping in view the importance of watershed development programme in rainfed areas, it is utmost realized by the project implementing agencies that the local people or ultimate beneficiaries of watershed programme should participate in the soil and water conservation programme. Therefore, it is realized to measure the extent of people's participation in soil and water conservation programme as well as extent of participation in different stages of soil and water conservation programme.

The study will describe and analyze the extent of people's participation in the particular programme of Integrated Wasteland Development Programme, Antisar watershed (Kapadvanj Taluka). The most important significance of the study would be that based on the findings to suggest an appropriate participatory approach in watershed management for sustainable agricultural production. It is hoped that the findings of the study will be very useful to planners, administrators, and extension functionaries to restructure and reframe the watershed development programme in future in right direction for the benefit of rural farmers.

## 3.3 JUSTIFICATION OF THE SAMPLE

The village rural farmers and farm women are directly or indirectly dependent on soil and water in the catchment area of a watershed. A sufficient care needs to be taken on the orientation, skill upgradation and motivation of the rural farmers towards soil and water conservation programme. The knowledge of rural farmers should be improved regarding adoption of soil and water conservation practices. The soil and water conservation programme on watershed management basis is developed by the rural farmers, for the rural farmers and of the rural farmers.

It was felt that without people's participation no soil and water conservation programme would be successful. There is a considerable role of local rural farmers to take decisions at the time of planning of SWC programme. To make the soil and water conservation programme successful, the local farmers should take care and protect the soil and water conservation structures in adverse situations. Therefore, the present study was planned to take the rural farmers and farm women of Antisar watershed as a sample of the study. All the farmers residing in the Antisar watershed or farmers having land in the Antisar watershed are taken as a sample of the present study. The sample of farmers for this study is very much justified because these farmers will be very much affected with the soil and water conservation programme for sustainable agricultural development through adopting watershed management practices. The farmers are the ultimate beneficiaries of the SWC programme.

The study was planned to be conducted in the Antisar watershed area purposively. Because the Antisar watershed development programme was sanctioned by Ministry of Rural Area Employment to the Central Soil & Water Conservation Research & Training Institute, Research Centre, Vasad and the investigator also employed in the Research Centre, Vasad. Antisar watershed area comes under Kapadvanj Taluka of Kheda district in Gujarat. The watershed is about 12 km from Kapadvanj.

## 3.4 JUSTIFICATION OF THE VARIABLES

### GENDER

Men and women both are having different capabilities to carry out different household and agricultural works efficiency. The women have more capabilities by nature to do some cultivation works more efficiently than the men and vice-versa. For example in agricultural enterprise the most of the business work such as buying inputs and selling of products are carried out by men only. Women are mostly doing the on farm activities such as seedbed preparation, interculture, weeding, harvesting of crops etc. The gender is an important variable, which affect the different activities in agriculture. Most of the decisions in planning of agricultural cultivation operations are taken by men. The women are to follow the decisions taken by the men in the rural areas. Therefore, gender variable is justified for the present study to find out whether the majority of decisions in planning of SWC programme is taken by men or not and also the extent of active participation by men as well as women in implementation and maintenance of soil and water conservation structure on their farm.

Varma and Sinha (1992) conducted a study on involvement of women and men in cultivation of crops.

The findings of the study indicated that involvement of men and women in various operations of Bajra cultivation showed that mean score of women's work load was higher than men's work load in high, medium, low socio-economic strata as well as in the pooled data. There was significant inter sex variation in high, low socio-economic strata and among the pooled data.

## AGE

Age is also a variable, which may be associated with adoption of soil and water conservation practices. The farmers, who are younger, may have less knowledge regarding Soil and Water Conservation practices, whereas old age farmers may have more experience and more knowledge level regarding SWC practices. As the age increases the practical knowledge and experiences regarding adoption of SWC practices also increases. The younger group of farmers may participate more in the soil and water conservation programme by contributing more labour work than the older one. The younger group of farmers may have good physical strength to do hard work during construction of soil and water conservation structures than the older farmers.

## SOCIO-ECONOMIC STATUS (OVERALL)

Many investigators stated that the socio-economic status of farmers directly or indirectly is correlated with the development of agriculture. The socio-economic status includes size of land holding, education, house, occupation, caste, farm power, material possession and family income. The socio-economic status variable was selected to know the effectiveness of socio-economic power possessed by the farmers on participation in soil and water conservation programme. The socio-economic status directly represents the physical infrastructure facilities and farm power possessed by individual farmer to carry out different SWC structures in their fields. The farmers having poor socio economic status are usually less capable to know and adopt new improved agricultural innovations, as compared to the farmers having high socio-economic status. The high socio-economic status farmers are already aware about new soil and water conservation technologies. Therefore, the farmers having high socio-economic status may be easily motivated to adopt soil and water conservation technologies. The variable socio-economic status of farmer is very much justified in the study, because it shows the capacity of farmer to contribute the available physical facilities such as implements, equipment, material etc. during implementation of soil and water conservation programme. Which may affect the participation of farmers in soil and water conservation programme.

## SOCIO-ECONOMIC STATUS (SPECIFIC INDICATORS)

### (i) Land holding :

Soil and Water Conservation technologies are adopted on the basis of contour lines of the land. Most of the technologies are adopted collectively by the large number of farmers on watershed catchment area basis. The large size of land holdings are very conducive for adoption of SWC practices. Therefore, the farmers having large size land holdings may easily adopt soil and water conservation technologies due to suitability of conservation structures to their land. The big farmers may participate and contribute more in soil and water conservation programme by adopting the soil and water conservation practices.

The farmers having small land holdings may not be able to adopt easily the soil and water conservation practices. The SWC practices are adopted on the basis of contour lines of watershed catchment area. Therefore, the conservation practices are adopted beyond the boundaries of farmers land holdings. Hence, land holdings also may affect the adoption of soil and water conservation technology.

### (ii) Education :

The academic achievement can reflect the mental ability of the farmers. In rural villages a varying levels of education standards are found. The high education level of farmers may find them easier to grasp knowledge and importance of soil and water conservation technologies. The educated farmers and farm women can easily be trained and motivated for their participation in SWC programme. The educated farmers and farm women are seems to be quite open-minded to exchange their ideas with each other. The educated farmers may also contribute their experiences by decision making ability in planning of soil and water conservation programme.

Rakholia (1996) reported that in case of beneficiaries of watershed programme, the increasing education had influence on the level of knowledge about soil and water conservation. While, in case of non-beneficiaries the increasing education had no influence on level of knowledge about soil and water conservation.

Therefore, education was considered as a variable for the present study.

### (iii) Farm Power :

Farm power was selected as a variable. It is a major asset needed for cultivation of agricultural crops. Farm power includes different agricultural machines, irrigation facilities, farm implements and also drought animals to carry out different cultivation operation on the land. Without the help of agricultural machines like tractor, trailer, different kinds of ploughs, cultivators etc., the construction of SWC structure would not be possible. Therefore, the farm power is an essential requirement of the farmers for participation in SWC programmes.

### (iv) Material possession :

The farmers having more materials may be exposed more to soil and water conservation programmes. In such situations, it is very easy to transfer the soil and water conservation technologies. The farmers having television, radio, tape recorder may have more opportunities to learn about SWC programme by watching different agricultural development programmes telecast on television or listening to radio programme. Many researchers revealed that the audio-visual aids had impact on learning behaviour of rural farmers. The rural families, who use more of television, radio, magazines etc. tend to be more knowledgeable than the other farmers.

Ingole *et. al.* (1993) also reported that the rural viewers preferred television mainly as an entertaining purpose (86%) followed by other purposes like education (61%), advertisement (36%) and information (15%).

### (v) Family size :

The respondents of Antisar watershed may vary in the size of their family. The farmers and farm women may belong to larger or small families in the rural area. The larger families may have more labour hands to works on their farms. The large family interactions are also useful in exchanging the knowledge and skills regarding soil and water conservation among the members of family. On the other hand, the small family may have less number of persons to work on their agricultural land. The larger family may provide more labour power to farmers for participation in the rural soil and water conservation programme.

### (vi) Family Income :

The farmers and farm women differ in the total income of their family. The farmers and farm women from high income families may have more resources and implements to help in adoption of soil and water conservation technologies. The farmers having more family income can contribute more money in construction of soil and water conservation structures in their watershed area. The farmers having more resources viz., implement, materials, machines etc., they can provide their resources to the soil and water conservation project implementing agency as their contribution of participation. The high economic status of a family also helps to learn more about soil and water conservation technologies by having more information sources.

## SOCIAL PARTICIPATION

The farmers and farm women having more contacts with rural social organizations may be interested in rural development programmes. Social participation is a voluntary contribution of services by a farmer or a farm woman to the village institution like; Panchayat, Co-operative Societies, Youth club, Anganawadi etc. as a member or office-bearer. It is understood that, if a farmer or farm woman participate or have more contacts with social institutions, can contribute or participate more in soil and water conservation programme by contributing labour, money, guidance, resources, experiences etc.

The similar findings were also reported by Rakholia (1996) that there was positive and significant association between level of knowledge of soil and water conservation programme beneficiaries and their social participation.

Chaudhary (1996) also observed that social participation was positive and significantly correlated with the adoption of soil and water conservation practices by the farmers.

## RISK PREFERENCE

The farmers and farm women differ in their ability to take risk in agricultural occupation. In rural area some farmers are willing to take risk in adoption of entirely new improved agricultural practices to earn more. On the other hand some farmers hesitate to adopt agricultural innovations. The high adopter farmers, who without any hesitation adopt new technology as soon as they come to know about new technology. There are also low adopter farmers, who do not try any new agricultural technology unless most other farmers have adopted them with success. The farmers having high risk taking ability may exhibit more participation in implementation of soil and water conservation programme by adopting new improved soil and water conservation technologies.

## KNOWLEDGE REGARDING SWC TECHNOLOGIES

If a farmer or farm woman has more knowledge regarding soil and water conservation technologies, it helps in easy adoption of SWC technologies by him/her. The farmers having good knowledge of SWC practices, may help in teaching and guiding other farmers in adoption and encourage participation in Soil Water Conservation programme. The farmers and farm women having experiences in practicing different soil and water conservation technologies on their fields, may participate more in soil and water conservation programme and share their experiences with other farmers.

Padmaiah (1997) reported that knowledge level of farmers regarding soil and water conservation practices has positive significant relationship with adoption of soil and water conservation technologies.

## ATTITUDE TOWARDS SWC PROGRAMME

Farmers and farm women may vary in their attitude towards SWC programme. Farmers having more favourable attitude towards SWC programme may participate more often in planning, implementation and maintenance of SWC programme.

The farmers with favourable attitude may also contribute more ideas and suggestions in the planning of such natural resource conservation programmes. The farmers having more favourable attitude towards soil and water conservation programme may adopt easily different soil and water conservation practices by contributing more labour, equipment, money etc.

Reddy (1987) also revealed that majority of farmers had more favourable attitude towards (i) soil and water conservation (ii) improved dry farming technologies (iii) non-arable land development of watershed development programme. He also found that big farmers had more favourable attitude than small farmers towards watershed development programme.

## ADOPTION OF SWC TECHNOLOGIES

Adoption behaviour varies from person to person, according to their knowledge and understanding. Some people accept innovations and put them into practices quickly, while some others are slow to put innovations in practice. Adoption of innovations also depends on situation and needs of the ultimate user.

Adoption of soil and water conservation practices depends on knowledge and resources available with the farmers. The farmers differ in their knowledge, understanding and resources possession. The farmers having sufficient knowledge regarding SWC practices as well as sufficient resources availability may provide conducive situation to adopt soil and water conservation practices. Therefore, the adoption of soil and water conservation practices by farmers is affected by the availability of resources such as mechanical power, farm implements, material possession, land holding etc. Therefore, the variable adoption of soil and water conservation practices was selected for the present study.

Bhutiya (1993) observed that majority (70%) of the farmers were found in medium adoption category, followed by high level adoption category (30%), and none in low category of adoption with respect to watershed management programme.

## 3.5 OBJECTIVES OF THE STUDY

This study was undertaken to find out the extent of people's participation in watershed management and impact of selected independent variables on the people's participation in watershed management. The study was taken up with the following specific objectives :

I) To study the overall extent of people's participation in soil and water conservation programme in the Antisar watershed.

II) To study the extent of people's participation in planning of soil and water conservation programme in the Antisar watershed.

III) To study the extent of people's participation in implementation of soil and water conservation programme in the Antisar watershed.

IV) To study the extent of people's participation in maintenance of soil and water conservation programme in the Antisar watershed.

V) To study the relationship between the overall extent of people's participation in soil and water conservation programme and the following variables:

1. Gender
2. Age

3. Socio-economic status (overall)
4. Socio-economic status (specific indicators):
   i) Family Land holding
   ii) Education
   iii) Farm power
   iv) Family size
   v) Family income
5. Social participation
6. Risk preference
7. Knowledge regarding SWC technologies
8. Attitude towards SWC programme
9. Adoption of SWC technologies

VI) To study the relationship between the extent of people's participation in planning of soil and water conservation programme and the following variables:

1. Gender
2. Age
3. Socio-economic status (overall)
4. Socio-economic status (specific indicators):
   i) Family Land holding
   ii) Education
   iii) Farm power
   iv) Family size
   v) Family income
5. Social participation
6. Risk preference
7. Knowledge regarding SWC technologies
8. Attitude towards SWC programme
9. Adoption of SWC technologies

VII) To study the relationship between the extent of people's participation in implementation of soil and water conservation programme and the following variables:

1. Gender
2. Age
3. Socio-economic status (overall)
4. Socio-economic status (specific indicators):
   i) Family Land holding
   ii) Education

       iii) Farm power
       iv) Family size
       v) Family income
5. Social participation
6. Risk preference
7. Knowledge regarding SWC technologies
8. Attitude towards SWC programme
9. Adoption of SWC technologies

**VIII)** To study the relationship between the extent of people's participation in maintenance of soil and water conservation programme and the following variables:

1. Gender
2. Age
3. Socio-economic status (overall)
4. Socio-economic status (specific indicators):
    i) Family Land holding
    ii) Education
    iii) Farm power
    iv) Family size
    v) Family income
5. Social participation
6. Risk preference
7. Knowledge regarding SWC technologies
8. Attitude towards SWC programme
9. Adoption of SWC technologies

**IX)** To study the constraints faced by the farmers and farm women during development of soil and water conservation programme of Antisar watershed.

**X)** To suggest an appropriate participatory approach for sustainable agricultural production in watershed management.

## ASSUMPTIONS

**I)** The rural farmers and farm women participate in planning, implementation and maintenance of soil and water conservation programme in Antisar watershed.

**II)** The rural farmers and farm women vary in their following traits:
1. Gender
2. Age
3. Socio-economic status (overall)

4. Socio-economic status (specific indicators):
    i) Family Land holding
    ii) Education
    iii) Farm power
    iv) Family size
    v) Family income
5. Social participation
6. Risk preference
7. Knowledge regarding SWC technologies
8. Attitude towards SWC programme
9. Adoption of SWC technologies

## NULL HYPOTHESES

I) There will be no significant relationship between the overall people's participation in soil and water conservation programme and the following variables:

1. Gender
2. Age
3. Socio-economic status (overall)
4. Socio-economic status (specific indicators):
    i) Family Land holding
    ii) Education
    III) Farm power
    iv) Family size
    v) Family income
5. Social participation
6. Risk preference
7. Knowledge regarding SWC technologies
8. Attitude towards SWC programme
9. Adoption of SWC technologies

II) There will be no significant relationship between the extent of people's participation in planning of soil and water conservation programme and the following variables.

1. Gender
2. Age
3. Socio-economic status (overall)
4. Socio-economic status (specific indicators):
    i) Family Land holding
    ii) Education

iii) Farm power
   iv) Family size
   v) Family income
5. Social participation
6. Risk preference
7. Knowledge regarding SWC technologies
8. Attitude towards SWC programme
9. Adoption of SWC technologies

III) There will be no significant relationship between the extent of people's participation in implementation of soil and water conservation programme and the following variables:

1. Gender
2. Age
3. Socio-economic status (overall)
4. Socio-economic status (specific indicators):
   i) Family Land holding
   ii) Education
   iii) Farm power
   iv) Family size
   v) Family income
5. Social participation
6. Risk preference
7. Knowledge regarding SWC technologies
8. Attitude towards SWC programme
9. Adoption of SWC technologies

IV) There will be no significant relationship between the extent of people's participation in maintenance of soil and water conservation programme and the following variables:

1. Gender
2. Age
3. Socio-economic status (overall)
4. Socio-economic status (specific indicators):
   i) Family Land holding
   ii) Education
   iii) Farm power
   iv) Family size
   v) Family income
5. Social participation

6. Risk preference
7. Knowledge regarding SWC technologies
8. Attitude towards SWC programme
9. Adoption of SWC technologies

## LIMITATIONS

The study has been undertaken as a research project and consequent upon the time and other resources available with the investigator, the following are the limitations of the study:

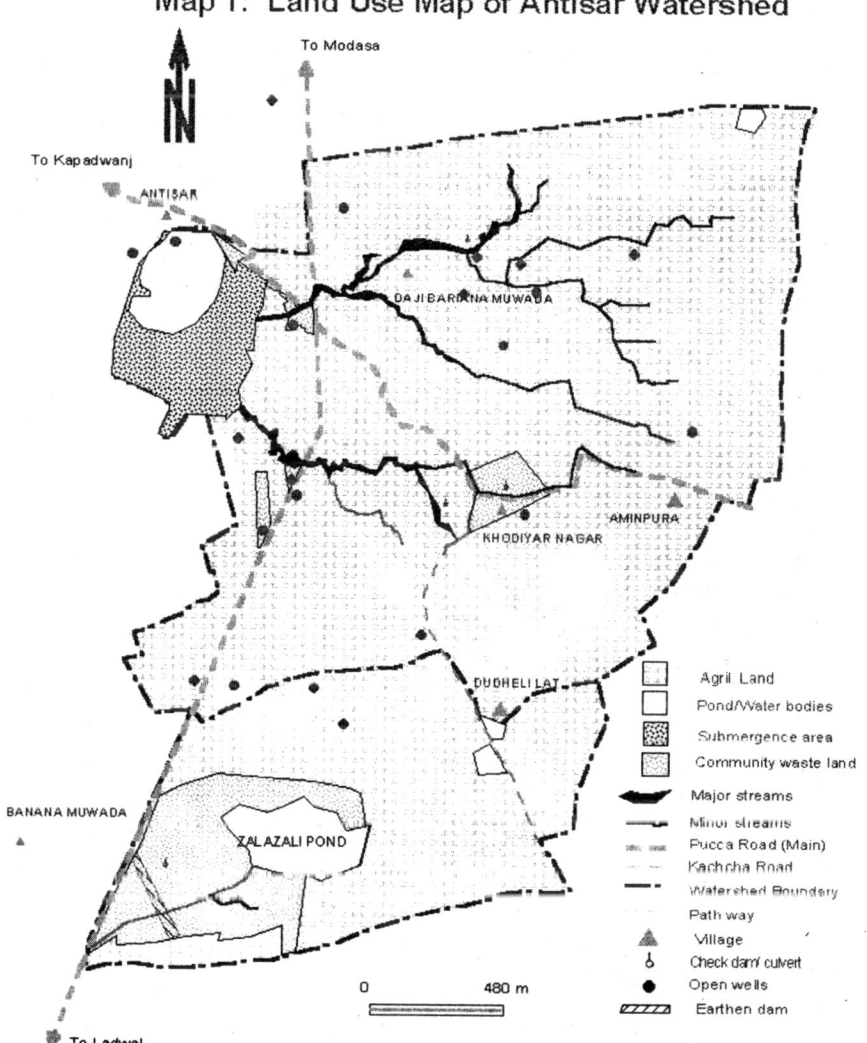

Map 1: Land Use Map of Antisar Watershed

1. The study is delimited to the farmers and farm women of the Antisar watershed.
2. The study of people's participation in soil and water conservation programme in Antisar watershed is delimited to the following phases of the programme:
   i) Programme planning
   ii) Programme implementation
   iii) Programme maintenance

## 3.6 METHODOLOGY

The present study aimed at studying people's participation in soil and water conservation for sustainable agricultural production on watershed basis. The present chapter discusses the locale of the study, pilot study, population of the study, the research design, construction of tools for data collection, scoring and categorization of data and statistical methods used for measuring independent and dependent variables. Thus, this chapter takes care of the scientific procedures adopted for the present investigation to draw rational, logical and meaningful inferences. The methodology followed for conducting the present study is reported in the following heads:

3.6.1 Locale of the study
3.6.2 Pilot study
3.6.3 Population of the study
3.6.4 Research design
3.6.5 Research tools for data collection
3.6.6 Validity of research tools
3.6.7 Reliability of the tools
3.6.8 Collection of data
3.6.9 Categorization and scoring of variables
3.6.10 Statistical analysis

### 3.6.1 LOCALE OF THE STUDY

National watershed development projects for rainfed areas were launched by the Government of India under different Five Year Plans. An Integrated Wasteland Development Project (IWDP) was sanctioned by Ministry of Rural Areas and Employment, Department of Wasteland Development, New Delhi, Government of India, to Central Soil and Water Conservation Research and Training Institute, Research Centre, Vasad, in March 1997. The scientific staff of this research centre, Vasad, decided to develop the Antisar watershed through the sanctioned Integrated Wasteland Development Project because the Antisar watershed was not adopted earlier by any other government agency to carry out soil and water conservation works for sustainable agricultural production.

The Antisar watershed is spread over 812 hectares of land. Out of that 736 hectares belong to individual farmers and 76 hectares is owned by Panchayat community/Government. The Antisar watershed is located at $73^0$ 10' E longitude and $23^0$ 0' N latitude and 30 mt. above mean sea level. Antisar watershed is located on Dakor-Pankhiya road about 100 km north of Vasad, comes under Kapadvanj Taluka of Kheda district in Gujarat. The watershed is about 12 km from Kapadvanj town (Map 1).

The Antisar watershed comprises of ten villages/hamlets namely, Aminpura, Antisar, Daji-bariya-na-muwada, Dudheli Lat, Kapadivav, Khodiyar Nagar, Motipura, Navafarm, Sukhpura and Vijaynagar. The total population of the watershed comprises of 1362 adults and 533 children. Most of them are Patel, Desai (Rabari), Bariya, Vankar, Parmar, Solanki, Zala and Vasava.

The present study was conducted in the Integrated Wasteland Development Project (IWDP), Antisar watershed purposively, because the Antisar watershed development programme was sanctioned by the Ministry of Rural Area Employment to the Central Soil and Water Conservation Research and Training Institute, Research Centre, Vasad. Moreover, the investigator is also employed in the Research Centre, Vasad. The investigator was interested to study the extent of people's participation in soil and water conservation under Antisar watershed development programme by both the male and female farmers.

### 3.6.2 PILOT STUDY

A pilot study was conducted in Antisar watershed area to measure the feasibility of the study entitled "people's participation in soil and water conservation programme for sustainable agricultural production in Antisar watershed of Gujarat" and feasibility of different variables included in the study. A sample of thirty rural farmers, comprised of 21 male and 9 female farmers was selected randomly from the Antisar watershed area for the purpose. The responses of the respondents were recorded by the investigator on the developed interview schedule by the interview method. The scoring of the different responses of the respondents was done accordingly. The quantitative responses of different variables were categorized and analyzed to assess the different variables included in the study.

The investigator tried to judge the feasibility of the study in the following terms through pilot study :

(i) Cooperation of rural male and female farmers during data collection.
(ii) Ability of rural farmers to respond to the interview schedule.
(iii) Time required by respondent in responding to the interview schedule.
(iv) Extent of mobility possible within the watershed area.
(v) Availability of variation in the variables included in the study.

**The pilot study helped in finding out the following :**

(i) The farmers of Antisar watershed area were cooperative and showed interest in the research study.

(ii) The rural male and female farmers of Antisar watershed understood the language of the tools prepared for data collection and were able to respond to the questions and statements of the tools.

(iii) The approximate time spent on data collection tools by interviewing one respondent was one and half-hours.

(iv) The transport and mobility within the watershed area was possible. The villages/hamlets of the watershed area were well connected by roads.

(v) There was variation among the respondents in relation to all the variables included in the present study.

### 3.6.3 POPULATION OF THE STUDY

The Integrated Wasteland Development Programme (IWDP), taken up at Antisar in Kapadvanj Taluka of Kheda district, Gujarat, was sanctioned by Ministry of Rural Areas and Employment, Government of India to Central Soil and Water Conservation Research and Training Institute, Research Centre, Vasad. The IWDP Antisar watershed has adopted a participatory approach of development as per the guidelines for national watershed development project for rainfed areas issued from Ministry of Rural Areas Employment, Government of India. According to watershed guidelines an Antisar Watershed Development society was formed of all the male and female farmers possessing land in the watershed area. An Antisar Watershed Development Committee was formed from the elected members of the Antisar watershed development society. The Antisar Watershed Development Committee has an elected chairman. The society was registered at Assistant Registrar of Societies, Nadiad, by application with formulated set of guidelines for strategies, rules, norms and funding pattern in respect of soil and water conservation works. The society was registered as Antisar Jalastrav Vikas Society (ANJVIS) in 1998. According to the guidelines of National Watershed Development Project for Rainfed Areas (NWDPRA), different types of groups were formed before commencing the development activities. The different groups were formed from the local farmers of the watershed area. The names of the groups were given as per the developmental activities to be carried out in the Antisar watershed. The Antisar watershed society had made different groups of farmers for their active participation in different development activities. Almost all the members of the watershed society were involved in the activities of the following groups:

**Users groups:**

a) Bunding and land levelling

b) Water management

c) Animal husbandry development
   d) Agricultural development
   e) Horticulture development
   f) Forestry development

**Self-help groups:**
   a) Grazing and protection
   b) Home business development
   c) Marketing management

The population of the study consisted of all the farmers and farm women who possessed land in the Antisar watershed area. All the members of Antisar Watershed Development Society including men and women were considered as the respondents for the study. All the 392 respondents comprised of 284 male farmers and 108 female farmers of Antisar watershed development society. Since, the size of the population in watershed area was small, therefore, all the farmers as well as farm women were considered as the sample for the study. Hence, it was a population study. The villagewise distribution of the respondents included in the study is presented in Table 1.

**Table 1: Villagewise distribution of the respondents in Antisar watershed.**

| | | | | N = 392 |
|---|---|---|---|---|
| Sr. No. | Name of Village | Respondents | | |
| | | Male (%) N = 284 | Female (%) N = 108 | Overall (%) N=392 |
| 1. | Antisar | 23.94 | 29.63 | 25.51 |
| 2. | Banana Muwada | 28.87 | 9.29 | 23.47 |
| 3. | Dajibariyana Muwada | 8.45 | 5.55 | 7.65 |
| 4. | Dudheli Lat | 22.53 | 46.29 | 29.09 |
| 5. | Khodiyar Nagar | 2.82 | 0.0 | 2.04 |
| 6. | Motipura | 13.38 | 9.25 | 12.24 |
| | Total | 100.00 | 100.00 | 100.00 |

### 3.6.4 RESEARCH DESIGN

Ex-Post-Facto research design was used for this study. Kerlinger (1976) stated that ex-post-facto research design is worthy to apply when the independent variables have already acted upon. Because the integrated watershed developmental works were already carried out in the Antisar watershed area for sustainable agricultural production. The ultimate beneficiary farmers had already participated in planning, implementation and maintenance of soil and water conservation programme in Antisar watershed. Hence, it was imperative to measure the extent of people's participation in the Antisar waterhed programme.

### 3.6.5 RESEARCH TOOLS FOR DATA COLLECTION

Interview schedule having seven sections was constructed as a tool for collection of data (Appendix II). The items of the interview schedule were prepared after the investigator :

(i) Visited the libraries of Indian Agricultural Research Institute, New Delhi, Gujarat Agricultural University, Campus Anand, WREMI, MSU, Baroda, ISRO, Ahmedabad for review of literature and discussion with subject matter specialists

(ii) Reviewed the books related to people's participation in rural development programmes.

(iii) Read research articles, which were related to the topic of the present study.

(iv) Reviewed other research studies related to the present study.

(v) Discussed with the subject matter specialists, soil and water conservationists and Extension experts.

(vi) Read the guidelines for watershed development programme issued by Ministry of Rural Development, Government of India.

**The tools constructed for the study were as follows:**

### Section I: Background information

The first section of the interview schedule consisted of a checklist of the socio-economic characteristics of the respondents.

The socio-economic characteristics of the respondents included in the study were as follows:

| VARIABLES | MEASUREMENT TOOLS |
|---|---|
| **Independent variables:** | |
| 1. Gender | Structured checklist prepared |
| 2. Age | Structured checklist prepared |
| 3. Socio-economic status (overall) | Standardized scale developed by Pareek and Trivedi (1963) was used with modifications. |
| 4. Socio-economic status (specific indicators) | Standardized scale developed by Pareek & Trivedi (1963) was used with modifications. |

| | | |
|---|---|---|
| i) | Family land holding | Structured checklist prepared |
| ii) | Education | Structured checklist prepared |
| iii) | Farm power | Structured schedule developed |
| iv) | Family size | Structured schedule developed |
| v) | Family income | Structured schedule developed |
| 5. | Social participation | The investigator developed structured schedule. The responses were asked to respondents as member or office-bearer of any rural social organization in past or present (Appendix II). |

## Section II: Risk Preference

The second section of the interview schedule consisted of a scale of the risk preference of the farmers in adoption of new improved soil and water conservation practices. The investigator developed a risk preference scale considering the following points:

(i) Adoption of new soil and conservation technologies in degraded wasteland.

(ii) Ability of farmers to adopt costly SWC practices.

(iii) Ability of farmers to replace old practices with new SWC practices.

The risk preference scale consisted of total ten statements. There were five negative and five positive statements.

## Section III: Knowledge regarding Soil and Water Conservation technologies

The third section of the interview schedule consisted of a knowledge test having fourteen open end type questions on soil and water conservation technologies related to:

(i) Agronomic soil and water conservation technologies for management and sustainable crop cultivation in watershed area.

(ii) Engineering soil and water conservation technologies for control of soil erosion and sedimentation deposition.

(iii) Forestry soil and water conservation technologies for cultivation of trees on boundaries and on slope land to reduce soil erosion.

A scale was developed by the investigator to measure the knowledge level of farmers regarding soil and water conservation technologies. The scale consisted of fourteen statements, with equal number of negative and positive statements. The scale had two-point responses system as yes or no.

## Section IV: Attitude of respondents towards soil and water conservation programme

The fourth part of the interview schedule consisted of attitude scale towards development of SWC programme. A Likert type attitude scale was developed by the investigator to measure attitude of male and female respondent towards soil and water conservation programme. The scale consisted of thirteen attitude statements comprised of six negative and seven positive statements to measure the attitude of the rural male and female farmers towards:

(i) Participation in planning of soil and water conservation programme.

(ii) Participation in implementation of soil and water conservation programme.

(iii) Participation in maintenance of soil and water conservation programme.

The responses were sought on a three-point continuum as agree, neutral and disagree.

## Section V: Adoption of soil and water conservation technologies :

The fifth part of the questionnaire consisted of the adoption scale of the different soil and water conservation technologies related to (i) Agronomy (ii) Engineering and (iii) Forestry. An adoption scale having-three point response system was developed by the investigator.

## Section VI: People's participation in SWC programme :

Sixth part of the questionnaire consisted of three-point rating scale to measure extent of people's participation in different stages of soil and water conservation programme. It was divided into three parts according to three phases of watershed development programme such as planning, implementation and maintenance stages of rural development programme as follows:

(i) People's participation in programme planning stage.

(ii) People's participation in programme implementation stage.

(iii) People's participation in programme maintenance stage.

The scale consisted of thirty statements and equally divided into three sub-headings according to the three phases or stages of rural development programme as stated above.

## Section VII: Constraints faced by the respondents:

Seventh part of the tool consisted of two-point rating scale to study the constraints faced by the rural male and female farmers during development through participation in soil and water conservation programme of Antisar watershed. It consisted of total thirteen statements related to the following areas of constraints.

(i) Economical constraints
(ii) Technological constraints
(iii) Input availability constraints
(iv) Situational constraints

## 3.6.6 VALIDITY OF RESEARCH TOOLS

The whole set of data collection tools was translated into Gujarati language to facilitate the respondents to easily understand the quarries because all the respondents of the study area were from Gujarat.

**Content validity of the tools:**

The developed set of research tools was sent to different subject matter specialists for validation. The experts selected for validation of tools were senior subject matter specialists in the disciplines of soil and water conservation and extension and communication. The experts represented the following departments:

(i) Department of Extension and Communication in Faculty of Home Science, Maharaja Sayajirao University of Baroda
(ii) Water Resource Engineering and Management Institute (WREMI), Samiala.
(iii) Faculty of Engineering from Maharaja Sayajirao University of Baroda.
(iv) Extension Education Institute, Gujarat Agricultural University, Anand campus, Anand.
(v) Department of Extension, B.A. College of Agriculture, GAU, Anand.
(vi) Central Soil and Water Conservation Research and Training Institute, Dehradun.

The experts were requested to check the tools for their appropriateness for the following aspects:

(i) Content validity
(ii) Format
(iii) Response system
(iv) Language
(v) Suitability to the respondents

The suggestions of the experts were incorporated in the tools. It was found that the contents of the tools were according to the topic of the study and the language and response system were also suitable to the respondents of the study.

### 3.6.7 RELIABILITY OF THE TOOLS

Reliability of the developed set of tools was measured by the test-retest method.

Reliability of tools was measured on thirty rural farmers (i.e. comprised of 21 male and 9 female farmers) by administering test-retest method by keeping one month gap to check the reliability of the tools. The respondents were selected randomly from the members of Antisar watershed development society.

Coefficient of correlation between two sets of scores was computed to see the reliability of tools to measure the risk preference, knowledge regarding SWC technologies, attitude towards soil and water conservation programme, adoption of soil and water conservation technologies and people's participation in soil and water conservation programme. The coefficient of correlation (r-value) of the tools was found to be as follows:

| | Tool | Reliability coefficient |
|---|---|---|
| (i) | Risk preference | .87 |
| (ii) | Knowledge regarding SWC practices | .86 |
| (iii) | Attitude towards SWC programme | .89 |
| (iv) | Adoption of SWC practices | .93 |
| (v) | People's participation in SWC programme | .91 |
| (vi) | Overall | .89 |

Thus, the tools for data collection were found reliable.

### 3.6.8 COLLECTION OF DATA

The respondents were contacted personally at their work places or at their residences in an informal way and data were collected personally by the investigator. The responses of the respondents were tick marked by the investigator in the structured tools made for data collection.

The investigator was accompanied by a technical assistant, temporarily posted under Integrated Wasteland Development Project, Antisar watershed, who was well-versed with Gujarati language and also known to the area. The data collection was done during October, 2000 to February, 2001.

## 3.6.9 CATEGORIZATION AND SCORING OF VARIABLES

The scoring, categorization and measurement of all the independent and dependent variables were done as follows:

**INDEPENDENT VARIABLES:**

| Sr. No. | Variables | Range of score | Categories |
|---|---|---|---|
| 1. | Gender : | — | a) Male |
|  |  | — | b) Female |
| 2. | Age : | 18-30 years | a) Young |
|  |  | 31-50 years | b) Middle |
|  |  | above 51 years | c) Old |
| 3. | Socio-economic status : | <mean - S.D. | a) Low |
|  |  | mean ± S.D. | b) Medium |
|  |  | >mean + S.D. | c) High |
| 4. | Land holding : | upto 2.5 acres | a) Marginal |
|  |  | 2.51 to 5.00 acres | b) Small |
|  |  | 5.01 to 7.50 acres | c) Medium |
|  |  | 7.51 to 10.00 acres | d) Large |
|  |  | above 10.00 acres | e) Very large |
| 5. | Education : | 0 | a) Illiterate |
|  |  | 1 | b) Can read only |
|  |  | 2 | c) Can read and write |
|  |  | 3 | d) Primary |
|  |  | 4 | e) Secondary |
|  |  | 5 | f) Higher secondary |
|  |  | 6 | g) Graduate |
|  |  | 7 | h) Above graduate |
| 6. | House : | 0 | a) No own house/rented |
|  |  | 1 | b) Own hut |
|  |  | 2 | c) Own kutcha house |
|  |  | 3 | d) Own semi-pucca house |
|  |  | 4 | e) Own pucca house |
|  |  | 5 | f) Own Mansion |

| 7. | Occupation: | 1 | a) Labour |
| --- | --- | --- | --- |
|  |  | 2 | b) Business |
|  |  | 3 | c) Cultivation |
|  |  | 4 | d) Service |
| 8. | Caste: | 1 | a) Scheduled Caste |
|  |  | 2 | b) Scheduled Tribe |
|  |  | 3 | c) Backward caste |
|  |  | 4 | d) General caste |
|  |  | 5 | e) Dominant caste |
| 9. | Farm power: | <Mean − S.D. | a) Low |
|  |  | Mean ± S.D. | b) Medium |
|  |  | >Mean + S.D | c) High |
| 10. | Material possession: | <Mean − S.D. | a) Less |
|  |  | Mean ± S.D. | b) Average |
|  |  | >Mean + S.D. | c) More |
| 11. | Type of family: | Husband, wife and children | a) Nuclear family |
|  |  | Husband, wife, children, in-laws and relatives | b) Joint family |
| 12. | Size of family: | Upto 5 members | a) Small |
|  |  | 6-10 members | b) Medium |
|  |  | More than 10 members | c) Large |
| 13. | Income of the family: | Up to Rs. 25000 | a) Very low |
|  |  | Rs. 25001 to Rs. 50000 | b) Low |
|  |  | Rs. 50001 to Rs. 75000 | c) Medium |
|  |  | Rs. 75001 to Rs. 100000 | d) High |
|  |  | Above Rs.100000 | e) Very high |

**14. Social participation:** The variable social participation is important during development of soil and water conservation programme. Social participation is a voluntary contribution of services by a farmer or farm woman to village level institutions during their village development programme. It can be categorized into the following:

| Category | Score |
|---|---|
| a) No membership | 0 |
| b) Membership in one organization | 1 |
| c) Membership in more than one organization | 2 |
| d) Holding position in organization | 3 |

## PSYCHOLOGICAL VARIABLES:

**1. Risk preference:** It refers to the degree to which an individual rural farmer and farm woman is oriented towards the risk and uncertainty in adoption of soil and water conservation technologies for sustainable agricultural production in watershed management. Risk preference scale was developed by the investigator to measure the degree to which farmers and farm women were oriented towards risk and uncertainty and have a courage to face problems in agriculture, by adopting new improved soil and water conservation technologies.

The scale consisted of 10 statements, out of which second, fourth, sixth, eighth and tenth were negative and rest of the statements were positive. The scores for positive statements were assigned as:

i) 3 for agree
ii) 2 for undecided and
iii) 1 for disagree

Reverse scores were assigned for negative statements. The scale is appended in the Appendix II. The minimum and maximum obtainable scores were as:

| Variable | Minimum score | Maximum score |
|---|---|---|
| Risk preference | 10 | 30 |

The respondents were divided into low, medium and high categories on the basis of total score obtained by them as following method:

| Range of scores | Categories |
|---|---|
| <mean - S.D. | a) Low |
| mean ± S.D. | b) Medium |
| >mean + S.D. | c) High |

**Intensity indices of statements:** Intensity scores of each items of risk preference were calculated. The following ranges were decided to find out and analyze the intensity indices of risk preference statements towards adoption of soil and water conservation practices:

| Intensity index range | Risk preference level |
|---|---|
| 1.00 to 1.59 | Low risk preference |
| 1.60 to 2.59 | Moderate risk preference |
| 2.60 to 3.00 | High risk preference |

2. **Knowledge:** The researcher developed a knowledge test consisting of fourteen statements, out of which, seven were negative statements and seven were positive statements. For the correct answer one score and for the incorrect answer zero score was assigned. The possible minimum and maximum obtainable scores were as follows:

| Variable | Minimum score | Maximum score |
|---|---|---|
| Knowledge | 0 | 14 |

The respondents were grouped into the following categories as below:

| Range of score | Category |
|---|---|
| <Mean - S.D. | a) Low |
| Mean ± S.D. | b) Medium |
| >Mean + S.D. | c) High |

**Knowledge index:**

The knowledge index of farmers of Antisar watershed was worked out as follows:

$$K = \frac{X_1 + X_2 + X_3 + \ldots + X_n}{N} \times 100$$

where,

$K$ = knowledge index of a farmer
$X_1 + X_2 + X_3 + \ldots + X_n$ = marks obtained for correct answer
$N$ = maximum possible marks in the schedule

**Overall knowledge index:** The overall knowledge index of all the respondents included from Antisar watershed area was computed as follows.

$$\text{Overall knowledge index} = \frac{\sum_{i=1}^{N} K}{N}$$

where,

$K$ = Knowledge index for ith respondents
$N$ = Total number of respondents

3. **Attitude:** The attitude scale towards soil and water conservation programme was developed by the investigator. The responses were asked on a three-point continuum as agree, neutral and disagree. The scores were assigned as 3, 2 and 1 for positive attitude statements and reverse scoring was done for negative statements. The possible minimum and maximum scores were as under:

| Variable | Minimum score | Maximum score |
| --- | --- | --- |
| Attitude | 13 | 39 |

All the respondents were grouped into three categories on the basis of total score obtained by them as follows:

| Category | Range of scores |
| --- | --- |
| a) Unfavourable | <mean - S.D. |
| b) Neutral | mean + S.D. |
| c) Favourable | >mean + S.D. |

**Intensity indices of statements:**

Intensity index scores of each items or statement of attitude scale was calculated by sum of scores of all the persons on each attitude statement and divided by total number of respondents. The following ranges were decided to find out the intensity indices of attitude towards soil and water conservation programme:

| Attitude level | Range of intensity index |
| --- | --- |
| Unfavourable | 1.00 to 1.59 |
| Neutral | 1.60 to 2.59 |
| Favourable | 2.60 to 3.00 |

**Individual Attitude Score:**

The individual attitude score of a respondent is equal to sum of scale values obtained by respondent on all responses and divided by total number of responses. The individual attitude score of a respondent was also computed by following formula.

$$I.A.S. = \frac{\text{Sum of scale values obtained by respondent}}{\text{Total number of responses}}$$

where,

I.A.S. = Individual Attitude Score

The overall group attitude score towards soil and water conservation programme in Antisar watershed was also computed with the following formula:

$$\text{Group attitude score} = \frac{\sum_{i=1}^{N} A.Q.}{N}$$

Where,
    I.A.S. = Individual attitude score
    N = total number of respondents

4. **Adoption:**

The investigator prepared a three-point continuum structured adoption scale. It comprised of twelve practices related to soil and water conservation. The scores were assigned as 1, 2 and 3 for responses viz. not known, known but not adopting and adopting SWC practices respectively. Thus, total score secured by an individual for their responses was used to calculate the adoption behaviour towards SWC technologies. The possible minimum and maximum scores were as under:

| Variable | Minimum score | Maximum score |
|---|---|---|
| Adoption | 12 | 36 |

All the respondents were grouped into three categories on the basis of total score obtained by them as follows:

| | Categories | Range of scores |
|---|---|---|
| a) | Low adopters | <mean − S.D. |
| b) | Moderate adopters | mean ± S.D. |
| c) | High adopters | >mean + S.D. |

**Adoption intensity indices of statements:** Intensity indices of statements related to each technology adoption behaviour was calculated. On the basis of intensity indices, the respondents were categorized as follows.

| Intensity index range | Adoption level |
|---|---|
| 1.00 to 1.59 | Low adoption |
| 1.60 to 2.59 | Moderate adoption |
| 2.60 to 3.00 | High adoption |

**Adoption quotient (A.Q.):**

An adoption quotient was developed to compute the adoption score of individual farmer and also overall adoption level of farmers of Antisar watershed as follows:

$$A.Q. = \frac{\text{No. of SWC practices adopted}}{\text{No. of SWC practices recommended}} \times 100$$

where,

A.Q. = Adoption Quotient

Overall adoption level in the area was also worked out by calculating the arithmetic mean of the adoption quotients of all the respondents.

$$\text{Overall adoption level} = \frac{\sum_{i=1}^{N} A.Q.}{N}$$

where,

A.Q. = Adoption quotient of the respondents

N = Total number of respondents

## DEPENDENT VARIABLES

### People's participation:

A detailed structured three-point continuum scale was developed by the investigator to assess the extent of people's participation in soil and water conservation programme in the different stages. The people's participation of respondents was measured in the following stages of rural development programme:

1. People's participation in programme planning
2. People's participation in implementation of programme
3. People's participation in maintenance of soil and water conservation programme

The responses of the respondents were recorded in the specially developed three-point continuum scale viz., great extent, some extent and least extent. The scores were assigned as:

i) 3 for great extent
ii) 2 for some extent and
iii) 1 for least extent

The possible minimum and maximum obtainable scores of people's participation in different stages SWC programme were as follows:

| Variables | Minimum score | Maximum score |
|---|---|---|
| a) People's participation in planning | 10 | 30 |
| b) People's participation in implementation | 10 | 30 |
| c) People's participation in maintenance | 10 | 30 |
| d) Overall people's participation | 30 | 90 |

All the respondents were grouped into three categories on the basis of the total scores obtained by them in development of all the three stages of SWC programme as follows:

| Range of scores | Categories |
|---|---|
| <Mean − S.D. | a) Less participation |
| Mean ± S.D. | b) Moderate participation |
| >Mean + S.D. | c) More participation |

**Statement Intensity Index (SII):** Statement intensity indices were calculated for people's participation in planning, implementation and maintenance stages of soil and water conservation programme with following index:

$$SII = \frac{\sum_{i=1}^{N} x_i}{N}$$

where,

SII = Statement intensity index

$\sum_{i=1}^{N} x_i$ = Sum of total scores of $i^{th}$ respondents towards a statement.

N = Total number of respondents

The level of participation for each activity or statement was decided as following criteria:

| Range of SII | Participation level |
|---|---|
| 1.00 to 1.59 | Less participation |
| 1.60 to 2.59 | Moderate participation |
| 2.60 to 3.00 | More participation |

To measure the extent of people's participation in different stages of watershed programme the People's Participation Index (PPI) was developed by the investigator as follows:

### People's Participation Index (PPI):

$$PPI = \frac{\text{Mean Participation Score (P)}}{\text{Maximum Participation Score}} \times 100$$

where,

$$P = \frac{\sum_{i=1}^{N} X_i}{N}$$

where,

N = Total number of respondents

$$P_i = \sum_{i=1}^{K} (PP_j + PI_j + PM_j)$$

where,

$PP_j$ = Total scores of people's participation in programme planning.
$PI_j$ = Total scores of people's participation in programme implementation.
$PM_j$ = Total scores of people's participation in programme maintenance.
K = Total number of statements on which responses of the respondents were recorded.

### 3.6.10 STATISTICAL ANALYSIS

The following statistical tests were used in the present research study.

1. **Percentage:** Simple interpretations were made on the basis of frequency and percentage.

2. **Mean:** The mean was obtained by dividing the sum of scores by the total number of respondents.

3. **Standard Deviation (S.D.):** The standard deviation was obtained by the square root of the average of the square deviation from mean.

4. **Pearson's coefficient of correlation(r):** The most often used and most precise coefficient of correlation is known as the Pearson product-moment coefficient of correlation (r). Coefficient of correlation was used to find out the relationship between each of the independent variable and the dependent variables by employing following formula (Best & Kahn, 1999):

$$r = \frac{N \cdot \sum XY - (\sum X) \cdot (\sum Y)}{\sqrt{N \cdot \sum X^2 - (\sum X)^2} \sqrt{N \cdot \sum Y^2 - (\sum Y)^2}}$$

Where, X = independent variables
Y = dependent variables
åX = sum of the X scores
åY = sum of the Y scores
åX² = sum of the squared X scores
åY² = sum of the squared Y scores
åXY = sum of the products of paired X and Y scores
N = number of paired scores

5. **Point Biserial Correlation:** To compute the coefficient of correlation between independent variable gender and different dependent variables, the Point Biserial correlation was used. The formula for point biserialr is (Ferguson, 1981):

$$r_{pbi} = \frac{X_p - X_q}{S_x} \sqrt{Pq}$$

In this formula $s_x$ is the standard deviation of scores on the continuous variable, defined as $(X - X)^2/N$. If the continuous variable is a test, $s_x$ is the standard deviation of test scores. The quantities of the dichotomous variable. If the dichotomous variable is a test item, p is the proportion of individuals who pass the item and q is the proportion who fail. $X_p$ and $X_q$ are the mean scores on the continuous variable of individuals within the two categories. Again, if the continuous variable is a set of test scores. $X_p$ is the mean score of those who pass the item and $X_q$ is the mean score o those who fail.

6. **Spearman ranks coefficient of correlation $p^{(rho)}$:** To compute the correlation between ranks assigned by male and female farmers towards constraints faced by them during development of Antisar watershed by adopting soil and water conservation practices. To compute the spearman rank order coefficient of correlation, the following simple formula was used (Best & Kahn, 1999):

$$p = 1 - \frac{6 \text{å} D^2}{N(N^2 - 1)}$$

where,
- D = the difference between paired ranks
- D² = the sum of the squared differences between ranks
- N = number of paired ranks

## 3.7 FINDINGS

The findings of the study are presented in this chapter as follows:

3.7.1 Profile of the respondents.

3.7.2 Risk preference of rural male and female farmers towards adoption of soil and water conservation technologies.

3.7.3 Knowledge level of rural male and female farmers regarding soil and water conservation technologies.

3.7.4 Attitude of rural male and female farmers towards soil and water conservation programme.

3.7.5 Adoption behaviour of rural male and female farmers towards soil and water conservation technologies.

3.7.6 Overall people's participation in soil and water conservation programme.

3.7.7 People's participation in planning of soil and water conservation programme.

3.7.8 People's participation in implementation of soil and water conservation programme.

3.7.9 People's participation in maintenance of soil and water conservation programme.

3.7.10 Relationship between independent variables and dependent variables.

3.7.11 Constraints faced by rural male and female farmers in development of Antisar watershed programme.

### 3.7.1 PROFILE OF THE RESPONDENTS

The people's participation in integrated watershed development through soil and water conservation programme is influenced by different characteristics of rural male and female farmers. It is beyond the scope of the present study to include all the characteristics of the rural male and female farmers. However, on the basis of the review of literature and observations carried out during the pilot study, some important characteristics are identified and analyzed. The findings related to characteristics of rural farmers are presented in the following pages.

**Gender:**

The Table 2 reveals that little less than the three-fourth of the respondents were male, whereas, little more than the one-fourth of them were female.

## Table 2: Distribution of respondents according to their gender.

N=392

| Sr. No. | Gender | Respondents (%) |
|---|---|---|
| 1. | Male | 284 (72.45) |
| 2. | Female | 108 (27.55) |
| | Total | 392 (100.00) |

**Age:**

## Table 3: Distribution of respondents according to their age.

N=392

| Sr. No. | Age group | Respondents | | Overall (%) |
|---|---|---|---|---|
| | | Male (%) N=284 | Female (%) N=108 | N=392 |
| 1. | Young age (18 to 30 years) | 19.01 | 47.22 | 26.78 |
| 2. | Middle age (31 to 50 years) | 72.53 | 50.00 | 66.33 |
| 3. | Old age (>50 years) | 8.46 | 2.78 | 6.89 |
| | Total | 100.00 | 100.00 | 100.00 |

The table 3 shows that about the two-third of the respondents, both male and female belonged to the middle age and little more than the one-fourth of them were young and few of them were in their old age.

The table 3 further reveals that more than seventy per cent of the male respondents were in their middle age and about the one-fifth of them were in their young age. Hardly 8.46 per cent of the male respondents belonged to old age group. Whereas, fifty per cent of the female respondents were found to be in their middle age and little less than fifty per cent of them were in their young age. A few of the female respondents belonged to old age group.

**Socio-economic status:**

It is seen from the table 4 that as the study revealed about three fourth (75.51%) of both male and female respondents belonged to a medium socio-economic status, while the remaining one fourth of them belonged to low or high socio-economic status (about 13.78 and 10.71 respectively).

The table also gives percentage of the male and female sections of the respondents separately. According to it, 72.53 per cent of the male respondents belonged to the medium socio-economic status. They were followed by 16.90

per cent of them belonging to the low socio-economic statues and 10.57 per cent of them belonging to the high socio-economic status. Among, 83.33 per cent of the female respondents belonged to the medium socio-economic status. They were followed by 11.11 per cent of them belonging to the high socio-economic status and 5.56 per cent of them belonging to the low socio-economic status.

**Table 4: Distribution of respondents according to their socio-economic status.**

N=392

| Sr. No. | Socio-economic status | Respondents | | Overall (%) |
|---|---|---|---|---|
| | | Male (%) N=284 | Female (%) N=108 | N=392 |
| 1. | Low status (<25.571 scores) | 16.90 | 5.56 | 13.78 |
| 2. | Medium status (25.571 to 51.821 scores) | 72.53 | 83.33 | 75.51 |
| 3. | High status (>51.821 scores) | 10.57 | 11.11 | 10.71 |
| | Total | 100 | 100 | 100 |
| | Mean =38.696 | SD = 13.125 | | |

**Land holding:**

**Table 5: Distribution of respondents according to their size of land holding.**

N=392

| Sr. No. | Size of land holding (acres) | Respondents | | Overall (%) |
|---|---|---|---|---|
| | | Male (%) N=284 | Female (%) N=108 | N=392 |
| 1. | Marginal land holder (<2.5 acres) | 14.08 | 5.55 | 11.73 |
| 2. | Small land holder (2.5 to 5.00 acres) | 30.28 | 33.33 | 31.12 |
| 3. | Medium land holder (5.1 to 10.00 acres) | 45.07 | 52.78 | 47.19 |
| 4. | Large land holder (10.1 to 20.00 acres) | 6.34 | 2.79 | 5.36 |
| 5. | Very large land holder (>20.00 acres) | 4.23 | 5.55 | 4.59 |
| | Total | 100.00 | 100.00 | 100.00 |

The Table 5 above shows that overall, among the respondents, both male and female, some 47.19 per cent of them were medium land holders. Next to them were one third small land holders who were 31.12 per cent of the total. One fifth of them belonged to either marginal, large or very large categories of land holders, 11.73%, 5.36% and 4.59% respectively.

However, according to the gender-based picture as laid down in the Table 5 and projected in the figure 5, little less than fifty per cent of the male respondents were medium level land holders, while 30.28 per cent i.e. less than the one third were small land holders, 14.08 per cent of them were marginal land holders. Group of large and very large land holders comprised hardly ten per cent of the total (6.34% and 4.23% respectively). Among the female respondents, more than fifty per cent (52.78%) belonged to the category of medium land holders. They were followed by small land holders as one third of the total (33.33%). Hardly, ten per cent of them belonged to the category of marginal, large and very large land holders (5.55%, 2.79% and 5.55% respectively).

**Education:** Since education is a vital determinant in the study, the level of education among the respondents was studied. The data are presented in Table 6.

**Table 6: Distribution of respondents according to their education.**

N=392

| Sr. No. | Education level | Respondents Male (%) N=284 | Female (%) N=108 | Overall (%) N=392 |
|---|---|---|---|---|
| 1. | Illiterate | 14.79 | 13.88 | 14.54 |
| 2. | Primary | 47.18 | 30.56 | 42.60 |
| 3. | Secondary | 33.88 | 50.00 | 38.27 |
| 4. | Graduate | 4.23 | 5.56 | 4.59 |
|  | Total | 100.00 | 100.00 | 100.00 |

The table 6 shows that of the total little more than forty per cent of male and female respondents (42.60%) had obtained primary education. Those with secondary education were less than forty per cent (38.27%). Whereas, the illiterate comprised 14.54 per cent and the literate with graduation were hardly 4.59 per cent of the total.

To put the data on the educational level gender-wise, the table 6 above shows that less than fifty per cent of the male respondents had obtained education upto primary level (47.18%). Those having education upto secondary level were almost the one third (33.88%). The illiterates among the male respondents were 14.79 per cent, while the literate with education upto graduation were 4.23 per cent of the total. In case of the female respondents, fifty per cent of them had studied upto secondary level, and those with primary education were about the one third (30.56%). The illiterate female respondents were 13.88 per cent and those with graduate level education were 5.56 per cent.

The review of the data reveals one striking fact that level of education was found to be bit higher among the female respondents than that among the male respondents. Particularly, considerably much higher number of the female respondents obtained education upto secondary level. More surprisingly, more of them had ventured to study upto the degree level. This fact may serve as striking feature to determine woman farmers' ability to participate in rural development activities.

House:

Table 7: Distribution of respondents according to their type of house.

N=392

| Sr. No. | Type of house | Respondent | | Overall (%) |
|---|---|---|---|---|
| | | Male (%) N=284 | Female (%) N=108 | N=392 |
| 1. | No own house | 2.81 | 0.0 | 2.04 |
| 2. | Own hut | 1.40 | 33.33 | 10.20 |
| 3. | Own kachcha house | 69.72 | 30.55 | 58.93 |
| 4. | Own semi-pucca house | 10.56 | 36.11 | 17.60 |
| 5. | Own pucca house | 15.49 | 0.0 | 11.22 |
| | Total | 100.00 | 100.00 | 100.00 |

The data presented in the table 7 above indicate that overall about sixty per cent of the male and female respondents (58.93%) owned kachcha houses. Some 17.60 per cent of them were staying in their own semi-pucca houses. About 11.22 per cent of them could afford their own pucca houses and the 10.20 per cent owned a hut. About 2.04 per cent of the total male and female respondents did not have their own houses.

The table 7 further shows that more than two third of male respondents (69.72) had their own kachcha houses. They were followed by some 15.49 per cent of them having their own pucca houses. While some 10.56 per cent owned semi-pucca houses and very low percentage of them did not own a house or a hut, say 2.80 per cent and 1.40 per cent respectively. More than one third of the female respondents (36.11%) had their own semi-pucca houses, about one third of them (33.33%) had their own huts and a little less than the one third of them

(30.55%) owned kuchcha houses. None of the female respondents possessed their own pucca houses or no houses.

**Occupation:**

Table 8: Distribution of respondents according to their occupation.

N=392

| Sr. No. | Occupation | Respondent | | Overall (%) |
|---|---|---|---|---|
| | | Male (%) N=284 | Female (%) N=108 | N=392 |
| 1. | Cultivation | 83.80 | 100.00 | 88.27 |
| 2. | Labour | 16.20 | 0.0 | 11.73 |
| 3. | Business | 0.0 | 0.0 | 0.0 |
| 4. | Service | 0.0 | 0.0 | 0.0 |
| | Total | 100.00 | 100.00 | 100.00 |

The table 8 reveals that the majority of the male and female respondents (88.27%) were engaged in cultivation as their chief occupation, whereas hardly 11.73 per cent of them had taken up labour work for their livelihood. None of the respondents had chosen business or service as their occupation.

The table 8 further shows that majority of the male respondents (83.80%) had taken up cultivation as their main occupation and while less than twenty per cent of them (16.20%) were engaged in labour work for their livelihood. Further, surprisingly all the women respondents had chosen cultivation as their main occupation.

**Caste:**

Table 9: Distribution of respondents according to their caste.

N=392

| Sr. No. | Caste | Respondent | | Overall (%) |
|---|---|---|---|---|
| | | Male (%) N=284 | Female (%) N=108 | N=392 |
| 1. | Scheduled Caste | 1.41 | 0.0 | 1.02 |
| 2. | Scheduled Tribe | 2.81 | 0.0 | 2.04 |
| 3. | Backward caste | 65.49 | 30.55 | 55.27 |
| 4. | General caste | 30.29 | 69.45 | 41.07 |
| | Total | 100.00 | 100.00 | 100.00 |

The table 9 shows that more than fifty per cent of male and female respondents (55.27%) belonged to the backward castes, while less than fifty per cent of them (41.07%) belonged to the general caste. A very low percentage of the respondents belonged to the Scheduled Tribe and Scheduled Caste, (2.04% and 1.02% respectively).

The table 9 further shows that about two third of the male respondents (65.49%) belonged to the backward caste. They were followed by a little less than one third of them (30.29%) hailed from the general caste. Those belonging to the Scheduled Tribe and the Scheduled Caste were a few (2.81% and 1.41% respectively). In case of female respondents, the situation was found to be reverse. About seventy per cent of female respondents (69.45%) belonged to the general caste and the remaining thirty per cent of female respondent (30.55%) belonged to the backward caste. None of the female respondents hailed from the Scheduled Caste and the Scheduled Tribe.

**Farm power:**

Farm power is yet one more determinant to help the present study as it has direct bearing on a farmer's capacity of equipments to assist any developmental project. In this light, it is evident from the table 10 and the figure 10 that the less than the two third of the overall respondents (62.24%) possessed moderate farm power. Little less than one fourth of them (23.73%) having more farm power and only, 14.03 per cent of them owned less farm power.

As regards the gender based picture, the table 10 reveals further that more than sixty per cent of the male respondents (62.67%) owned moderate farm power, about one fifth of them (19.03%) had more farm power and little less than one fifth of them possessed less farm power. Talking about the female section, more than sixty per cent of them (61.11%) owned moderate farm power, more than one third of them (36.11%) had more farm power and only a few of the female respondents owned less farm power.

**Table 10: Distribution of respondents according to their category of farm power.**

N=392

| Sr. No. | Farm power | Respondent | | Overall (%) |
|---|---|---|---|---|
| | | Male (%) N=284 | Female (%) N=108 | N=392 |
| 1. | Less farm power (<4.78 scores) | 18.30 | 2.78 | 14.03 |
| 2. | Moderate farm power (4.78 to 12.79 scores) | 62.67 | 61.11 | 62.24 |
| 3. | More farm power (>12.79 scores) | 19.03 | 36.11 | 23.73 |
| | Total | 100.00 | 100.00 | 100.00 |
| | Mean = 8.792 | SD = 4.007 | | |

**Cattle possession:**

**Table 11: Distribution of respondents according to their cattle possession.**

N=392

| Sr. No. | Number of cattle | Respondent | | Overall (%) |
|---|---|---|---|---|
| | | Male (%) N=284 | Female (%) N=108 | N=392 |
| 1. | Having 1 to 2 cattle | 13.38 | 5.56 | 11.22 |
| 2. | Having 3 to 5 cattle | 72.54 | 91.67 | 77.81 |
| 3. | More than 5 cattle | 14.08 | 2.77 | 10.97 |
| | Total | 100.00 | 100.00 | 100.00 |

It is revealed from the table 11 above that overall more than the three fourth of both the male and female respondents (77.81%) owned 3 to 5 cattle. Those followed them with 1 to 2 cattle were just 11.22 per cent. However, some of the respondents (10.97%) owned more than 5 cattle.

The table further reveals that of the male respondents, about three fourth (72.54%) possessed 3 to 5 cattle, while some 14.08 per cent of them had more than 5 cattle and some 13.38 per cent of them owned just 1 to 2 cattle. Referring to the female respondents, a good majority of them (91.67%) owned 3 to 5 cattle and a few, say 5.56 per cent of them possessed 1 to 2 cattle. Those having more than 5 cattle were just negligible with 2.77 per cent.

**Mechanical power:**

**Table 12: Distribution of respondents according to their mechanical power.**

N=392

| Sr. No. | Mechanical power | Respondent | | Overall (%) |
|---|---|---|---|---|
| | | Male (%) N=284 | Female (%) N=108 | N=392 |
| 1. | Less mechanical power (<0.176 scores) | 20.42 | 5.56 | 16.33 |
| 2. | Medium mechanical power (0.176 to 3.812 scores) | 70.42 | 77.78 | 72.44 |
| 3. | More mechanical power (>3.812 scores) | 9.16 | 16.66 | 11.23 |
| | Total | 100.00 | 100.00 | 100.00 |
| | Mean = 1.994 | SD = 1.818 | | |

The table 12 shows that more than seventy per cent of the overall respondents owned medium mechanical power, while some 16.33 per cent of them had less mechanical power. However, some 11.23 per cent of them possessed more mechanical power.

However, as per the gender-wise picture, seventy per cent of the male respondents (70.42%) owned medium mechanical power, one fifth of them (20.42%) owned less mechanical power. Hardly, 9.16 per cent of them possessed more mechanical power. Whereas, in the case of female respondents, more than the three fourth of them (77.78%) had medium mechanical power, 16.66 per cent of the female respondents had more mechanical power and a few (5.56%) had less mechanical power.

### Irrigation facility:

**Table 13: Distribution of respondents according to the irrigation facilities available to them.**

N=392

| Sr. No. | Irrigation facilities | Respondent | | Overall (%) |
|---|---|---|---|---|
| | | Male (%) N=284 | Female (%) N=108 | N=392 |
| 1. | Less irrigation facilities (<0.164 scores) | 31.69 | 19.44 | 28.32 |
| 2. | Medium irrigation facilities (0.164 to 2.960 scores) | 47.89 | 25.00 | 41.58 |
| 3. | More irrigation facilities (>2.960 scores) | 20.42 | 55.56 | 30.10 |
| | Total | 100.00 | 100.00 | 100.00 |
| | Mean = 1.562 | SD = 1.398 | | |

The table 13 shows that overall more than forty per cent of the respondents enjoyed medium irrigation facilities, less than one third of them (30.10%) having more irrigation facilities and little more than the one fourth of the respondents (28.32%) did not avail adequate irrigation facilities for their agriculture.

The data presented in table 13 further show that less than fifty per cent of the male respondents had medium irrigation facilities to their command, while less than the one third of them (31.69%) had less irrigation facilities. Those to enjoy more irrigation facilities were almost one fifth of the male respondents.

Speaking of the female counterpart those enjoying more irrigation facilities were more than fifty per cent and one fourth of the female respondents had medium irrigation facilities. About the one fifth of them did not have adequate irrigation facilities.

**Implement Possession:**

**Table 14: Distribution of respondents according to their farm implement possession.**

N=392

| Sr. No. | Farm implement possession | Respondent | | Overall (%) |
|---|---|---|---|---|
| | | Male (%) N=284 | Female (%) N=108 | N=392 |
| 1. | Having no implement | 2.82 | 8.33 | 4.34 |
| 2. | Having 1 implement | 51.41 | 22.22 | 43.37 |
| 3. | Having 2 implements | 26.76 | 32.41 | 28.57 |
| 4. | Having 3 implements | 16.19 | 20.37 | 17.09 |
| 5. | More than 3 implements | 20.11 | 16.67 | 6.12 |
| | Total | 100.00 | 100.00 | 100.00 |

It is revealed from the data in the Table 14 above that overall little more than forty per cent of the respondents possessed only one implement, followed by more than the one fourth possessing two implements. Whereas, little less than twenty per cent possessed three implements.

Further, the gender-wise data revealed that about fifty per cent of the male respondents possessed only one implement. They were followed by little more than the one fourth of them (26.76%) possessing two implements. About the one fifth of them (20.11%) possessing more than three implements. While less than twenty per cent (16.19%) possessed three implements. Of the female respondents, almost the one third of them (32.41%) possessed two implements, followed by nearly one fifth of them (22.22%) possessing one implement. About one fifth of the female respondents (20.37%) possessed three implements and less than twenty per cent of them (16.67%) possessed more than three implements.

**Material possession:**

**Table 15: Distribution of respondents according to their household material possession.**

N=392

| Sr. No. | Material possession | Respondent | | Overall (%) |
|---|---|---|---|---|
| | | Male (%) N=284 | Female (%) N=108 | N=392 |
| 1. | Less materials (<2.06 scores | 33.09 | 8.33 | 26.27 |
| 2. | Average materials (2.06 to 6.83 scores) | 50.71 | 55.56 | 52.04 |
| 3. | More materials (>6.83 scores) | 16.20 | 36.11 | 21.70 |
| | Total | 100.00 | 100.00 | 100.00 |
| | Mean = 4.449 | SD = 2.384 | | |

The data presented in the table 15 show that more than fifty per cent of the overall respondents owned average material possession, little more than one fourth (26.27%) possessed less material possession and little more than the one fifth (21.70%) owned more household material possession.

The table further shows that little beyond fifty per cent of the male respondents (50.71%) owned average household material possession, almost the one third (33.09%) possessed less material possession and less than twenty per cent of them (16.20%) were had more material possession. In case of the female respondents, the situation is bit reverse, more than fifty per cent female respondents having average household materials possession. About more than the one third of them (36.11%) owned more material possession. Whereas, a few of the female respondents had less household material possession.

**Family size:**

The table 16 presents the data on family size. As revealed by it, about the two third of the overall respondents (64.54%) belonged to small sized families, one third of them (33.42%) belonged to medium sized families and a few of the respondents (hardly 2.04%) belonged to large sized families.

The table further shows that the two third of the male respondents (66.90%) belonged to small families. They were followed by less than the one third of them (30.28%) who belonged to medium sized families. While few of them (2.82%) belonged to large families. Likewise, among the female respondents about sixty per cent of them (58.33%) belonged to small families and little more than forty per cent of them (41.67%) lived to the medium sized families (figure 16).

**Table 16: Distribution of respondents according to their family size.**

N=392

| Sr. No. | Family size | Respondent | | Overall (%) |
|---|---|---|---|---|
| | | Male (%) N=284 | Female (%) N=108 | N=392 |
| 1. | Small family (Up to 5 members) | 66.90 | 58.33 | 64.54 |
| 2. | Medium family (6 to 10 members) | 30.28 | 41.67 | 33.42 |
| 3. | Large family (More than 10 members) | 2.82 | 0.0 | 2.04 |
| | Total | 100.00 | 100.00 | 100.00 |

**Type of family:**

**Table 17: Distribution of respondents according to their type of family.**

N=392

| Sr. No. | Type of family | Respondent | | Overall (%) |
|---|---|---|---|---|
| | | Male (%) N=284 | Female (%) N=108 | N=392 |
| 1. | Nuclear family | 42.96 | 29.44 | 36.20 |
| 2. | Joint family | 57.04 | 70.56 | 63.80 |
| | Total | 100.00 | 100.00 | 100.00 |

The data collected on type of family is presented in the table 17. It revealed that nearly two third of the overall respondents (63.80%) belonged to joint families, whereas about the one third of them (36.20%) belonged to nuclear families.

The table further shows that the male respondents little less than sixty per cent belonged to joint families and little more than forty per cent of them belonged to nuclear families. Whereas, about seventy per cent of the female respondents belonged to joint families and the remaining about thirty per cent of them belonged to nuclear families.

**Annual income:**

**Table 18: Distribution of respondents according to their annual income of family.**

N=392

| Sr. No. | Annual income category | Respondent | | Overall (%) |
|---|---|---|---|---|
| | | Male (%) N=284 | Female (%) N=108 | N=392 |
| 1. | Up to 25,000 | 83.10 | 72.22 | 80.10 |
| 2. | 25,001 to 50,000 | 11.97 | 16.67 | 13.26 |
| 3. | 50,001 to 75,000 | 0.71 | 2.78 | 0.27 |
| 4. | 75,001 to 100,000 | 1.40 | 2.78 | 1.78 |
| 5. | Above 100,000 | 2.82 | 5.55 | 3.57 |
| | Total | 100.00 | 100.00 | 100.00 |

The table 18 shows that majority of the overall respondents (80.10%) had annual income upto Rs. 25,000. Then followed those with 13.26 per cent of the respondents had the annual income ranging between Rs.25,001 to 50,000. Hardly six per cent of them had the annual earning beyond Rs.50,000 (i.e. 0.27 per cent upto Rs.75,000, 1.78 per cent upto Rs.1,00,000 and 3.57 per cent beyond Rs.1,00,000).

The table further shows that among the male respondents, the majority (83.10%) male respondents were earning upto Rs.25,000 annually, while some 11.90 per cent of them could earn ranging from Rs.25,001 to 50,000. Hardly about five per cent were earning beyond Rs.50,000. Speaking of the female respondents majority (72.22%) of them had annual income upto Rs.25,000. Some 16.67 per cent of them were having annual income between Rs.25,001 to Rs.50,000. While hardly ten per cent of female respondents had beyond Rs.50,000 annual income.

## Social participation:

**Table 19: Distribution of respondents according to their social participation.**

N=392

| Sr. No. | Social participation | Respondent | | Overall (%) |
|---|---|---|---|---|
| | | Male (%) N=284 | Female (%) N=108 | N=392 |
| 1. | Less participation (<.292 scores) | 15.49 | 55.56 | 26.53 |
| 2. | Moderate participation (0.292 to 3.124 scores) | 74.65 | 22.22 | 60.20 |
| 3. | More participation (>3.124 scores) | 9.86 | 22.22 | 13.27 |
| | Total | 100.00 | 100.00 | 100.00 |
| | Mean = 1.708 | SD = 1.416 | | |

The table 19 indicates that sixty per cent of the overall respondents had moderate level of social participation, about one fourth of them had less social participation and only 13.27 per cent of them rendered more social participation.

To spell it gender-wise, some three fourth of the male respondents rendered moderate social participation, fifteen per cent of them had less social participation and only about ten per cent had more social participation. Whereas, more than fifty per cent the female respondents rendered less social participation and little more than one fifth of them rendered moderate social participation and about same number of them rendered more social participation.

### 3.7.2 RISK PREFERENCE OF RURAL MALE AND FEMALE RESPONDENTS TOWARDS ADOPTION OF SWC TECHNOLOGIES

**Risk preference levels:**

**Table 20: Distribution of the respondents according to their levels of risk preference.**

N=392

| Sr. No. | Risk preference levels | Respondent | | Overall (%) |
|---|---|---|---|---|
| | | Male (%) N=284 | Female (%) N=108 | N=392 |
| 1. | Low risk preference (<18.43 scores) | 15.49 | 12.04 | 14.54 |
| 2. | Moderate risk preference (18.43 to 23.91 scores) | 67.61 | 57.40 | 64.80 |
| 3. | High risk preference (>23.91 scores) | 19.90 | 30.56 | 20.66 |
| | Total | 100.00 | 100.00 | 100.00 |
| | Mean = 21.174 | SD = 2.741 | | |

The table 20 explained that out of the total respondents, little less than the two third (64.80%) exhibited moderate risk preference regarding adoption of new soil and water conservation technologies. One fifth of them held high risk preference and about fifteen per cent of them showed low risk preference.

The table further projects a gender-wise picture of the risk preference. Little higher than the two third of the male respondents had moderate risk preference. About one fifth of male respondents exhibited high risk preference and about fifteen per cent of them held low risk preference. Whereas, on the part of the female respondents, 57.40 per cent exhibited moderate risk preference. Little less than the one third of them (30.56%) had high risk preference and while little more than ten per cent of them exhibited low risk preference. This picture projects the level of interest among the male and the female sections regarding the adoption of new soil and water conservation technologies.

**Risk preference of the rural male respondents towards SWC activities:**

**Table 21: Itemwise percentage distribution and intensity indices according to the risk preference of the rural male respondents.**

| Sr. No. | Items | A. | U.D. | D.A. | Intensity indices |
|---|---|---|---|---|---|
| | **POSITIVE ITEMS** | | | | |
| 1. | You would prefer to adopt new Soil and Water Conservation (SWC) technologies for production in degraded wasteland. | 87.50 | 12.50 | 00.00 | 2.87 |
| 2. | You would like to adopt SWC technologies in cultivable land at any cost for increasing production. | 84.37 | 9.38 | 6.25 | 2.78 |
| 3. | You would like to try an entirely new SWC technology in farming although it involves higher financial investment because it is sure to be highly productive. | 50.00 | 28.13 | 21.87 | 2.28 |
| 4 | Even if you fail in adoption of new SWC technology once, you would still like to try it once more. | 40.62 | 40.62 | 18.75 | 2.22 |

| | | | | | |
|---|---|---|---|---|---|
| 5. | You would prefer to try out new SWC technology, irrespective of it being successful or failure. | 28.12 | 37.50 | 34.38 | 1.93 |

**NEGATIVE ITEMS**

| | | | | | |
|---|---|---|---|---|---|
| 6. | You would like to adopt Soil and Water Conservation methods only when you are sure about the success in agriculture production. | 12.15 | 28.12 | 59.38 | 2.46 |
| 7. | You would like to adopt new SWC technology only after you verify about the success of the technology through results demonstrated at government research farms. | 25.00 | 15.63 | 59.37 | 2.34 |
| 8. | You would prefer to grow more crops than one in order to avoid total failure of crop. | 6.25 | 59.37 | 34.37 | 2.28 |
| 9. | You would try new Soil and Water Conservation methods only after most farmers have used them successfully. | 18.76 | 40.62 | 40.62 | 2.21 |
| 10. | You would like to continue with old technologies than adopting new SWC technologies about which you are not sure/ confident. | 34.38 | 15.62 | 50.00 | 2.15 |

The data in table 21 regarding risk preference are presented in descending order of itemwise intensity indices score. It reveals that the positive items with high intensity indices regarding the risk preference of the male respondents towards adoption of soil and water conservation technologies were as follows:

- *Adoption of new Soil and Water Conservation (SWC) technologies for production in degraded wasteland.*
- *Adoption of SWC technologies on cultivable land at any cost for increasing production.*

It means that the rural male respondents were highly positive about high risk preference. They showed their willingness to adopt new SWC technologies for sustainable agricultural development on watershed basis in degraded wasteland and cultivable land.

It is also seen from the table that the positive items with moderate intensity indices were as follows:

- *Trying out an entirely new SWC technology in farming which involves higher financial investment but it is highly productive.*
- *Even if one failed in adoption of new SWC technology first time, he/she would still try it out once more.*
- *One would prefer to try new SWC technology irrespective of it being successful or failure.*

The table shows that the male respondents showed moderate agreement on the point of surety of success of the SWC project.

The table also reveals that none of the rural male respondents showed low risk preference in the positive items towards adoption of new improved soil and water conservation technologies. It means that majority of the male respondents were in high and moderate agreement to adopt new improved soil and water conservation technologies on their watershed approach.

Table 21 further reveals that on negative items about the success of the project, considerable male respondents expressed their doubts. Hence, negative items with moderate intensity indices were as follows:

- *To adopt Soil and Water Conservation methods only, when one is sure about success in the agricultural production.*
- *To adopt new SWC technology only after one verifies about the success of the technology through results demonstrated at government research farms.*
- *To grow more crops than one in order to avoid total failure of crop.*
- *To try new Soil and Water Conservation methods only after most farmers have used them successfully.*
- *To continue with old technologies than adopting new SWC technologies about which you are not sure/confident.*

The rural male respondents showed moderate agreement on the above stated items with moderate risk preference towards these negative items for adoption of new SWC technologies for sustainable agricultural development on watershed basis.

**Risk preference of the rural female respondents towards SWC activities:**

**Table 22: Itemwise percentage distribution and intensity indices according to the risk preference of the rural female farmers.**

| Sr. No. | Items | A. | U.D. | D.A. | Intensity indices |
|---|---|---|---|---|---|
| | **POSITIVE ITEMS** | | | | |
| 1. | You would prefer to adopt new Soil and Water Conservation (SWC) technologies for production in degraded wasteland. | 92.86 | 7.14 | 0.0 | 2.93 |
| 2. | You would like to adopt SWC technologies in cultivable land at any cost for increasing production. | 85.71 | 7.14 | 7.14 | 2.79 |
| 3. | You would like to try an entirely new SWC technology in farming although involves higher financial investment because it is sure to be highly productive. | 64.29 | 28.57 | 7.14 | 2.57 |
| 4. | Even if you failed in adoption of new SWC technology once, you would still like to try it once more. | 35.71 | 35.71 | 28.57 | 2.07 |
| 5. | You would prefer to try out new SWC technology irrespective of it being successful or failure. | 35.71 | 21.43 | 42.86 | 1.92 |
| | **NEGATIVE ITEMS** | | | | |
| 6. | You would like to adopt new SWC technology only when you verify the success of the technology through the results demonstrated at government research farms. | 7.14 | 28.57 | 64.29 | 2.57 |
| 7. | You would like to continue with old technologies than | 14.28 | 28.58 | 57.14 | 2.43 |

| | | | | | |
|---|---|---|---|---|---|
| | adopting new SWC technologies about which you are not sure/confident. | | | | |
| 8. | You would prefer to grow more crops than one in order to avoid total failure of crop. | 0.0 | 57.14 | 42.86 | 2.42 |
| 9. | You would try new Soil and Water Conservation methods only after most farmers have used them successfully. | 14.28 | 35.72 | 50.00 | 2.35 |
| 10. | You would like to adopt Soil and Water Conservation methods only, when you are sure about success in agricultural production. | 21.43 | 42.86 | 35.71 | 2.14 |

The table 22 reveals that the female respondents showed a different trend in their responses to the SWC programmes. The intensity indices regarding the positive items indicate that they preferred highly to take risk by adopting the SWC technologies in the interest of improving their land base to render it more fertile and more productive:

- **To get production on degraded wasteland.**
- **To increase production on cultivable land at any cost.**

It means that the female respondents looked forward to reaping sustainable agricultural development on watershed basis and they showed eagerness and preference to run into risk of any kind, even if they have to put in huge finance. But for the bit weaker income base they exhibited moderate response as regards the financial involvement.

The table indicates that the positive items with moderate intensity indices were as follows:

- **To try an entirely new SWC technology in farming even if it involves higher financial investment because it is sure to be highly productive.**
- **Even if one failed in adoption of new SWC technology once, you would still like to try it once more.**
- **To try out new SWC technology irrespective of it being successful or failure.**

This shows that the rural female respondents moderately agreed with the above items and have moderate risk preference towards these positive items to adopt new costly SWC technologies for sustainable agricultural development on watershed basis.

The table 22 also reveals that none of the rural female respondents showed low risk preference for the adoption of new improved soil and water conservation technologies. It means that majority of the female respondents agreed highly and moderately with adoption of new improved soil and water conservation technologies on watershed approach.

The table further reveals that on the part of the female respondents, not a single of the negative items with high intensity index was recorded that would point at the risk preference of the female respondents towards adoption of soil and water conservation technologies. As well, none of the female respondents showed high agreement with negative items towards adoption of new soil and water conservation technologies. The negative items with moderate intensity indices were as follows:

- **You would like to adopt new SWC technology only when you verify the success of the technology through results demonstrated at government research farms.**
- **You would like to continue with old technologies than adopting new SWC technologies about which you are not sure/confident.**
- **You would prefer to grow more crops than one in order to avoid total failure of crop.**
- **You would try new Soil and Water Conservation methods only after most farmers have used them successfully.**
- **You would like to adopt Soil and Water Conservation methods only, when you are sure about the success in agricultural production.**

This means that the rural female respondents moderately agreed with the above items and have moderate risk preference towards adoption of new SWC technologies only when sure about success otherwise they would like to be continued with old technologies.

The table also reveals that none of the female respondents showed low risk preference on the negative items towards adoption of new improved soil and water conservation technologies. It means due to their selectively high and moderate risk preference, the female respondents seemed to show up a bit matured and sensible attitude to the cause of improvement in the agriculture.

### 3.7.3 KNOWLEDGE LEVELS OF RESPONDENTS REGARDING SOIL AND WATER CONSERVATION TECHNOLOGIES

**Knowledge levels of respondents:**

**Table 23: Percentage distribution of the respondents according to their knowledge levels regarding SWC technologies.**

N=392

| Sr. No. | Knowledge levels | Respondent | | Overall (%) |
|---|---|---|---|---|
| | | Male (%) N=284 | Female (%) N=108 | N=392 |
| 1. | Low (<5.40 scores) | 23.94 | 3.70 | 18.37 |
| 2. | Moderate (5.40 to 9.05 scores) | 67.61 | 76.85 | 70.15 |
| 3. | High (>9.05 scores) | 8.45 | 19.45 | 11.48 |
| | Total | 100.00 | 100.00 | 100.00 |
| | Mean = 7.230 | SD = 1.822 | | |

Table 23 and the figure 1 reflect that majority of the overall respondents (70.15%) knew moderately about the SWC technologies and 18.37 per cent of them had low knowledge about the SWC technologies. However, a very small section with 11.48 per cent of them had acquired considerable high knowledge regarding soil and water conservation technologies.

The table 23 and the figure 1 further reveal that little more than two third of the male farmers (67.61%) exhibited moderate level of knowledge regarding soil and water conservation technologies and little less than the one fourth of them possessing low level of knowledge. Only less than ten per cent of the male respondents possessed high level of knowledge. Among the female respondents majority (76.85%) had moderate level of knowledge, about one fifth of them (19.45%) possessed high level of knowledge and hardly 3.70 per cent of the female respondents had low level of knowledge regarding soil and water conservation technologies.

**Knowledge of the rural male and female farmers regarding soil and water conservation technologies:**

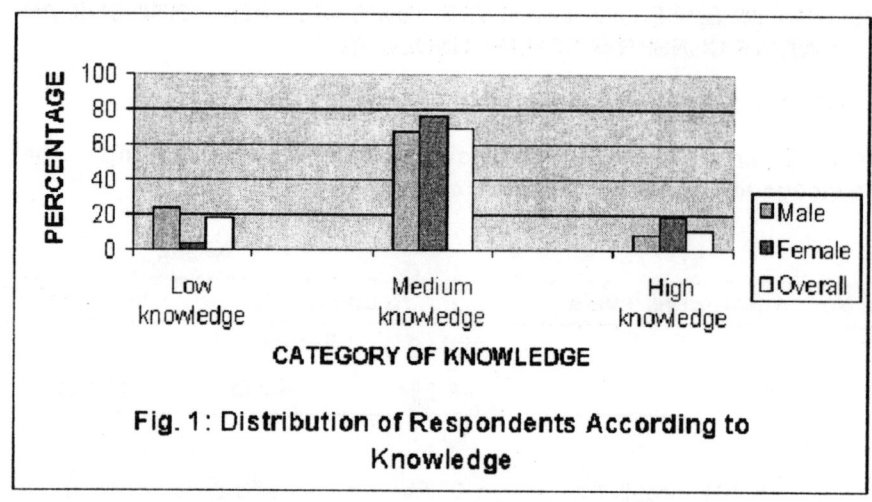

Fig. 1: Distribution of Respondents According to Knowledge

Table 24: Itemwise percentage distribution of the rural male and female farmers according to their knowledge regarding soil and water conservation technologies.

N=392

| Sr. No. | Items | Respondent Male (%) N=284 | Female (%) N=108 | Overall (%) N=392 |
|---|---|---|---|---|
| | **POSITIVE ITEMS** | | | |
| 1. | The mate appropriate soil condition for seed germination. | 92.25 | 94.44 | 92.86 |
| 2. | The trees are planted on the boundaries of crop fields. | 82.74 | 83.33 | 82.91 |
| 3. | The minimum ploughing is done to create appropriate soil condition for seed germination. | 64.43 | 56.48 | 62.24 |
| 4. | The animals can be allowed in the specific grazing land after adequate growth of vegetation. | 53.16 | 58.33 | 54.59 |
| 5. | The Cultivation of cereal crops is followed by pulse or leguminous crops. | 51.40 | 62.96 | 54.59 |

| | | | | |
|---|---|---|---|---|
| 6. | The crops are grown across the slope of the agriculture field. | 47.18 | 66.66 | 52.55 |
| 7. | The two or more crops are grown simultaneously for continuous land cover and protection from beating action of rains. | 45.07 | 63.88 | 50.25 |
| | **NEGATIVE ITEMS** | | | |
| 8. | One crop is grown repeatedly in cultivable land, year after year | 60.56 | 36.11 | 53.82 |
| 9. | In crop cultivation, cereal crops follow the cereal crops only. | 4.5.77 | 61.11 | 50.00 |
| 10. | The waterways used for conducting surface water in agricultural fields should not be covered with grasses. | 50.35 | 44.44 | 48.72 |
| 11. | The bunds are made along the slope of the sloppy land. | 44.36 | 50.00 | 45.92 |
| 12. | The crops with less canopy cover are grown to protect the soil from rain water erosion. | 30.98 | 52.77 | 36.98 |
| 13. | In the fallow fields, the stubble of crops are taken completely with roots. | 23.23 | 33.33 | 26.02 |
| 14. | The crops are grown along the slope of the land. | 23.24 | 19.44 | 22.19 |

### Table 24 reveals that:

I. A good majority of the respondents both the male and female, knew how to conserve soil and water, it was found that most of the male and female farmers have knowledge of the following practices:

- **The materials such as saw dust, straw, paddy husk, groundnut shell, crop residues, leaves etc. were spread on the surface of the land to protect the soil from erosion.**
- **The trees were planted on the boundaries of the crop fields.**

II. Among both the male and female respondents about fifty per cent of them were aware of the following improved SWC practices in farming:

- **The minimum ploughing is done to create appropriate soil condition for seed germination.**
- **The animals are allowed in the specific grazing land after adequate growth of vegetation.**
- **The cultivation of cereal crops is followed by pulse or leguminous crops.**
- **The crops are grown across the slope of the agriculture field.**
- **The two or more crops are grown simultaneously for continuous land cover and protection from beating action of rains.**

III. It was also found that about fifty per cent of the overall both the male and female respondents were aware of the following negative practices in farming:

- **One crop found to be grown repeatedly in cultivable land, year after year.**
- **In cultivation, cereal crops are taken following the cereal crops only.**

   **It shows that fifty per cent or more of the overall male and female respondents had knowledge of these soil and water conservation practices.**

IV. As regards the conservation of land and prevention of the land erosion about fifty percent of both male and female respondents were found to indulge in negative practices, which shows that they had negative thinking or wrong knowledge about the conservation of agricultural land in the following practices:

- **The waterways used for conducting surface water in agricultural fields should not be covered with grasses.**
- **The bunds are made along the slope of the sloppy land.**
- **The crops with less canopy cover are grown to protect the soil from rain water erosion.**
- **In the fallow fields, the stubble of crops are taken completely with roots.**
- **The crops are grown along the slope of the land.**

It may be noted here that the overall extent of knowledge level of both the male and female respondents was computed with the help of the developed knowledge index as explained in chapter 3 on the methodology. It was found to be 53.54 per cent, which was a moderate level. Whereas, the extent of knowledge among the male respondents was found to be 50.35 per cent and that of among the female respondents was found to be 56.74 per cent. Therefore, the extent of knowledge level among the female respondents was found to be higher than that among the male respondents.

### 3.7.4 ATTITUDE OF RURAL MALE AND FEMALE FARMERS TOWARDS SWC PROGRAMME:

**Attitude levels of respondents:**

Table 25: Distribution of the respondents according to their attitude levels towards participation in SWC programme.

N=392

| Sr. No. | Attitude | Respondent | | Overall (%) |
|---|---|---|---|---|
| | | Male (%) N=284 | Female (%) N=108 | N=392 |
| 1. | Unfavourable (<25.01 scores) | 16.90 | 13.89 | 16.07 |
| 2. | Neutral (25.01 to 30.30 scores) | 71.83 | 74.07 | 72.70 |
| 3. | Favourable (>30.30 scores) | 11.27 | 12.04 | 11.23 |
| | Total | 100.00 | 100.00 | 100.00 |
| | Mean = 27.657 | | SD = 2.647 | |

The table 25 and the figure 2 show that majority of the overall respondents (72.70%) had neutral attitude towards soil and water conservation programme, some 16.07 per cent of them had unfavourable attitude and more than ten per cent of the respondents (11.23%) exhibited favourable attitude.

It further shows that among the male respondents majority of them (71.83%) held neutral attitude towards soil and water conservation programme, followed about 16.90 per cent of them with unfavourable attitude and hardly 11.27 per cent of the male respondents showed favourable attitude towards SWC programme. Similarly, among the female respondents, majority of them (74.04%) held neutral attitude, followed by about 11.89 per cent of the female farmers with unfavourable attitude and 12.04 per cent had favourable attitude towards participation in SWC programme.

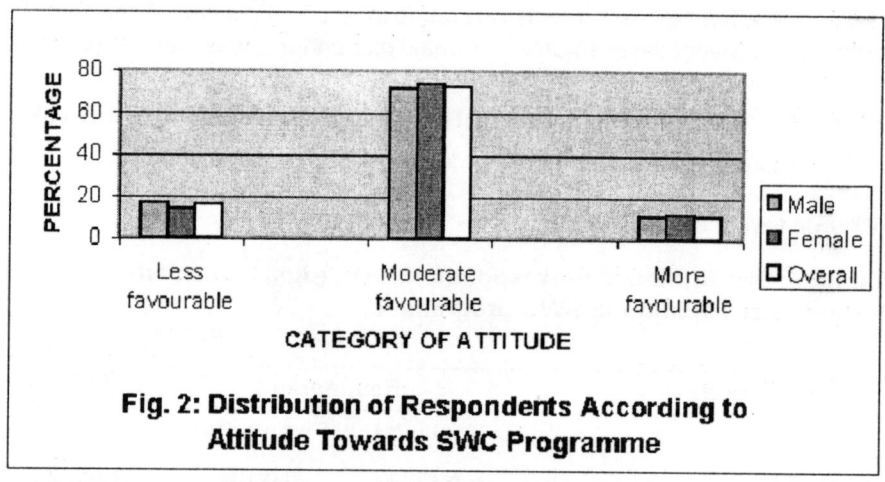

**Fig. 2: Distribution of Respondents According to Attitude Towards SWC Programme**

Attitude of the rural male farmers towards SWC programme:

Table 26: Itemwise percentage distribution and intensity indices according to the attitude of rural male farmers towards SWC programme.

| Sr. No. | Items | A.% | N.% | D.A.% | Intensity indices |
|---|---|---|---|---|---|
| | **POSITIVE ITEMS** | | | | |
| 1. | Farmers should contribute labour or money towards repair and maintenance of the SWC structures on their land. | 14.08 | 67.61 | 18.31 | 1.95 |
| 2. | Farmers should motivate their fellow farmers for collectively contribution in repair and maintenance of SWC structures. | 32.39 | 20.43 | 47.18 | 1.85 |
| 3. | Farmers should suggest any point of individual or collective interest in planning of SWC programme. | 2.82 | 64.79 | 32.39 | 1.70 |
| 4. | Farmers should contribute own labour or money in construction of SWC structures. | 9.86 | 50.00 | 40.14 | 1.69 |
| 5. | Farmers should maintain and repair their SWC structures | 15.49 | 8.45 | 76.06 | 1.39 |

| | | | | | |
|---|---|---|---|---|---|
| | from time to time with their own expenses. | | | | |
| 6. | Farmers should contribute materials or equipments in construction of SWC structures. | 5.63 | 26.76 | 67.61 | 1.38 |
| 7. | Farmers should participate in soil and water conservation (SWC) programme planning meetings. | 2.82 | 2.11 | 95.07 | 1.07 |
| | **NEGATIVE ITEMS** | | | | |
| 8. | Farmer's contribution of labour or money in construction of SWC structures is not required. | 35.91 | 34.51 | 29.58 | 1.93 |
| 9. | Farmers should not contribute labour or money to the government body PIA for repair of SWC structures. | 38.73 | 38.73 | 22.54 | 1.83 |
| 10. | PIA is totally responsible for construction of SWC structures in farmers' fields. | 42.25 | 36.62 | 21.13 | 1.78 |
| 11. | Women's participation in SWC programme planning meetings is inessential. | 55.63 | 12.68 | 31.69 | 1.76 |
| 12. | Maintenance and repair works should be done through PIA with the government money. | 40.84 | 44.37 | 14.79 | 1.73 |
| 13. | SWC structures should be constructed with the government money through project implementation agency (PIA). | 51.41 | 31.69 | 16.90 | 1.65 |

The table 26 reveals that not a single positive item on the attitude of the male respondents towards soil and water conservation programme was found to be having high intensity index. Thus, the male respondents did not show favourable attitude towards the positive items in soil and water conservation programme.

Low intensity indices were found for the male respondents for the following positive items:

- **Farmers should maintain and repair their SWC structures from time to time with their own expenses.**
- **Farmers should contribute materials or equipments in construction of SWC structures.**
- **Farmers should participate in soil and water conservation (SWC) programme planning meetings.**

This means that the male respondents showed unfavourable attitude towards these items and they showed unfavourable attitude towards contribution of materials in construction and maintenance of structures and also participation in planning meetings.

The male respondents showed neutral attitude for the rest of the positive items. It means that they were undecided about their contribution of labour or money towards construction and maintenance of SWC structures.

It is seen from the table 26 that not a single negative item was found with high intensity index that would reflect on the attitude of the male respondents towards soil and water conservation programme. Thus, the male respondents did not show favourable attitude towards negative items related to the soil and water conservation programme.

The table shows that the male farmers showed neutral attitude towards all the negative items. The male respondents did not show favourable and unfavourable attitude towards any negative item regarding soil and water conservation programme. It means that the male farmers were undecided about their contribution of labour or money is required or not in construction of structures.

**Attitude of rural female farmers towards SWC programme:**

**Table 27: Itemwise percentage distribution and intensity indices according to the attitude of rural female farmers towards SWC programme.**

N=108

| Sr. No. | Items | A.% | N.% | D.A.% | Intensity indices |
|---|---|---|---|---|---|
| | **POSITIVE ITEMS** | | | | |
| 1. | Farmers should contribute labour or money towards repair and maintenance of the SWC structures on their land. | 11.11 | 63.89 | 25.00 | 1.86 |
| 2. | Farmers should motivate their fellow farmers for collectively contribution in repair and maintenance of SWC structures. | 25.92 | 20.37 | 53.71 | 1.72 |

| | | | | | |
|---|---|---|---|---|---|
| 3. | Farmers should contribute own labour or money in construction of SWC structures. | 11.11 | 49.07 | 39.82 | 1.71 |
| 4. | Farmers should suggest any point of individual or collective interest in planning of SWC programme. | 0.0 | 51.85 | 48.15 | 1.52 |
| 5. | Farmers should contribute materials or equipment in construction of SWC structures. | 12.03 | 18.52 | 69.95 | 1.42 |
| 6. | Farmers should maintain and repair their SWC structures from time to time with their own expenses. | 9.26 | 3.71 | 87.03 | 1.22 |
| 7. | Farmers should participate in soil and water conservation (SWC) programme planning meetings. | 1.85 | 6.48 | 91.67 | 1.10 |
| | **NEGATIVE ITEMS** | | | | |
| 8. | SWC structures should be constructed with government money through project implementation agency (PIA). | 37.04 | 35.18 | 27.78 | 1.90 |
| 9. | Maintenance and repair works should be done through PIA with the government money. | 22.22 | 65.74 | 12.04 | 1.89 |
| 10. | Farmer's contribution of labour or money in construction of SWC structures is not required. | 45.37 | 40.74 | 13.89 | 1.68 |
| 11. | Women's participation in SWC programme planning meetings is inessential. | 55.55 | 23.15 | 21.30 | 1.65 |
| 12. | PIA is totally responsible for construction of SWC structures on farmers' fields. | 55.56 | 25.00 | 19.44 | 1.63 |
| 13. | Farmers should not contribute labour or money to the government body PIA for repair of SWC structures. | 52.78 | 36.11 | 11.11 | 1.58 |

The table 27 reveals that not a single positive item was found to be having high intensity index. Thus, the female respondents did not show favourable attitude towards any positive item regarding the soil and water conservation programme.

The female respondents had low intensity indices towards the following positive items:

- **Farmers should suggest any point of individual or collective interest in the planning of SWC programme.**
- **Farmers should maintain and repair their SWC structures from time to time with their own expenses.**
- **Farmers should contribute materials or equipments in construction of SWC structures.**
- **Farmers should participate in soil and water conservation (SWC) programme planning meetings.**

It means that the female respondents disagreed with these positive items and they showed unfavourable attitude towards these items regarding participation in planning meetings and contribution of materials towards construction and maintenance of SWC structures.

The female respondents showed neutral intensity indices with the rest of the positive items, this indicates that the female respondents showed neutral attitude towards contribution of labour and money in construction and maintenance of SWC structures.

The table 27 further shows that not a single negative item was found with high intensity index. It means that the female respondents did not show favourable attitude towards the any negative item regarding the soil and water conservation programme.

It is seen from the table 27 that only one negative item was found having low intensity index. It was, "SWC structures should be constructed with the government money through the project implementation agency (PIA)". It means that the female respondents disagreed with the item and they showed unfavourable attitude towards this negative item.

The table shows that the female respondents showed neutral attitude towards rest of the negative items. It means that the female respondents were undecided or neutral towards the contribution of labour or money is required or not in construction and maintenance of SWC structures.

### 3.7.5 ADOPTION OF SOIL AND WATER CONSERVATION TECHNOLOGIES BY RURAL MALE AND FEMALE FARMERS

**Extent of adoption of SWC technologies:**

Table 28: Distribution of the respondents according to their levels of adoption of SWC technologies.

N=392

| Sr. No. | Adoption levels | Respondent | | Overall (%) |
|---|---|---|---|---|
| | | Male (%) N=284 | Female (%) N=108 | N=392 |
| 1. | Low (<21.37 scores) | 11.97 | 19.45 | 14.03 |
| 2. | Medium (21.37 to 28.28 scores) | 81.69 | 74.07 | 79.59 |
| 3. | High (>28.28 scores) | 6.34 | 06.48 | 6.38 |
| | Total | 100.00 | 100.00 | 100.00 |
| | Mean = 24.826 | | SD = 3.456 | |

The table 28 and the figure 3 show that majority of the respondents (79.59%) were medium level adopters. They were followed by some 14.03 per cent of them who were low level adopters and hardly 6.38 per cent of them were high level adopters as regards the soil and water conservation technologies.

The table further shows that majority of the male respondents (81.69%) were medium level adopters. Then followed some 11.97 per cent of them who were low level adopters and hardly 6.34 per cent of them who were high level adopters. Likewise, among the female respondents about the three fourth of them (74.07%) were medium level adopters. They were followed by nearly one fifth of the female respondents (19.45%) who were low level adopters and some 6.48 per cent of them who were high level adopters of the soil and water conservation technologies.

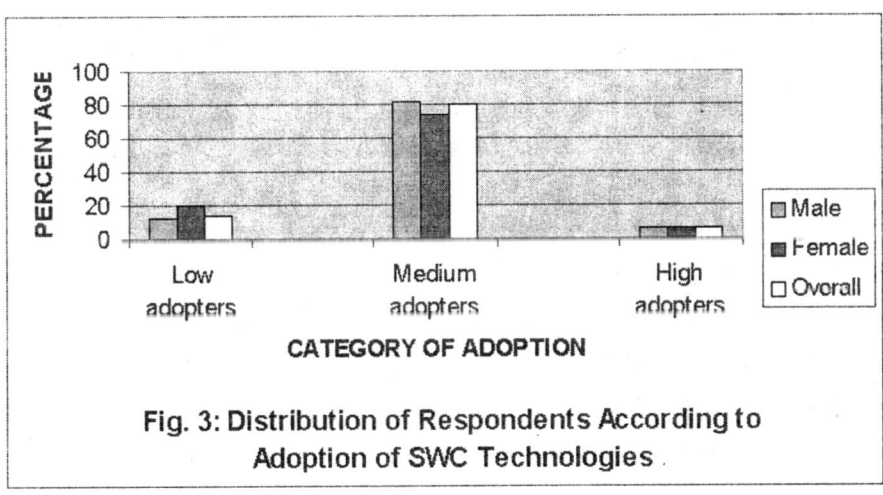

Fig. 3: Distribution of Respondents According to Adoption of SWC Technologies.

## Adoption of male farmers according to SWC technologies:

**Table 29: Percentage distribution and intensity indices according to the adoption of different SWC technologies by rural male farmers.**

N=284

| Sr. No. | Technology | Responses | | | Intensity indices |
|---|---|---|---|---|---|
| | | Not known % | Known but not adopted % | Adopted % | |
| 1. | Contour farming | 26.76 | 45.07 | 28.17 | 2.01 |
| 2. | Intercropping | 3.52 | 69.01 | 27.46 | 2.23 |
| 3. | Cover cropping | 13.38 | 55.63 | 30.98 | 2.17 |
| 4. | Mulching | 13.38 | 34.50 | 52.11 | 2.38 |
| 5. | Summer ploughing | 6.34 | 14.08 | 79.58 | 2.73 |
| 6. | Land levelling | 16.20 | 53.52 | 29.58 | 2.11 |
| 7. | Contour bunding | 59.15 | 35.21 | 5.63 | 1.46 |
| 8. | Marginal bund | 16.20 | 68.31 | 15.49 | 1.99 |
| 9. | Terracing | 33.10 | 53.52 | 13.38 | 1.80 |
| 10. | Checkdam | 13.38 | 52.11 | 34.51 | 2.21 |
| 11. | Gully plug | 38.03 | 38.03 | 23.94 | 1.85 |
| 12. | Farm pond | 21.83 | 59.86 | 18.31 | 1.96 |

The table 29 shows that the intensity indices for adoption of soil and water conservation practices as derived from the responses of the male respondents. It ranged from 1.46 to 2.73. At its top, the male respondents showed high intensity index, i.e. 2.73 in the adoption of summer ploughing. The male respondents showed moderate level of adoption in the following SWC practices in the descending order as indicated below:

- Mulching (2.38)
- Intercropping (2.23)
- Checkdam (2.21)
- Cover cropping (2.17)
- Land levelling (2.11)
- Contour farming (2.01)

- Marginal bund (1.99)
- Farm pond (1.96)
- Gully plug (1.85)
- Terracing (1.80)

They however, showed low intensity index with 1.46 in adoption of the SWC practice like contour bunding.

The table further shows that the overall adoption level of male respondents remained at 69.56 per cent which shows higher adoption level. It shows that the farmers of the Antisar watershed area held high adoption towards SWC technologies for sustainable agricultural production.

**Adoption of female farmers according to SWC technologies:**

Table 30: Percentage distribution and intensity indices according to the adoption of different SWC technologies by rural female farmers.

N=108

| Sr. No. | Technology | Not known % | Known but not adopted % | Adopted % | Intensity indices |
|---|---|---|---|---|---|
| 1. | Contour farming | 21.30 | 46.30 | 32.40 | 2.11 |
| 2. | Intercropping | 12.96 | 65.74 | 21.30 | 2.08 |
| 3. | Cover cropping | 21.30 | 62.96 | 15.74 | 1.94 |
| 4. | Mulching | 10.18 | 37.96 | 51.85 | 2.41 |
| 5. | Summer ploughing | 11.11 | 8.33 | 80.56 | 2.69 |
| 6. | Land levelling | 26.85 | 43.52 | 29.63 | 2.07 |
| 7. | Contour bunding | 54.63 | 32.41 | 12.96 | 1.58 |
| 8. | Marginal bund | 33.33 | 50.00 | 16.67 | 1.83 |
| 9. | Terracing | 32.41 | 59.26 | 8.33 | 1.75 |
| 10. | Checkdam | 8.33 | 36.11 | 55.56 | 2.47 |
| 11. | Gully plug | 39.81 | 32.41 | 27.78 | 1.87 |
| 12. | Farm pond | 8.33 | 75.00 | 16.67 | 2.08 |

The table 30 shows the intensity indices for adoption of soil and water conservation technologies as derived from the responses of the female respondents. It ranges from 1.58 to 2.69. The female respondents showed high intensity index 2.69, only in the adoption of summer ploughing. The female respondents showed moderate level of adoption for the following soil and water conservation practices in the descending order indicated as follows:

- Checkdam (2.47)
- Mulching (2.41)
- Contour farming (2.11)
- Intercropping (2.08)
- Farm pond (2.08)
- Land levelling (2.07)
- Cover cropping (1.94)
- Gully plug (1.87)
- Marginal bund (1.83)
- Terracing (1.75)

They however, showed low risk preference with 1.58 in adoption of the SWC practice like contour bunding.

The overall adoption level of female respondents was found to be 66.58 per cent. The computation was done with the help of the developed adoption index. Therefore, the overall adoption level of the female respondents was also found to be in the category of higher adoption level. This shows that the female farmers of the Antisar watershed area too held high adoption of SWC technologies for sustainable agricultural production.

### 3.7.6 OVERALL PEOPLE'S PARTICIPATION IN SOIL AND WATER CONSERVATION PROGRAMME

Table 31: Distribution of the respondents according to their overall people's participation levels in SWC programme.

N=392

| Sr. No. | Overall people's participation levels | Respondent Male (%) N=284 | Female (%) N=108 | Overall (%) N=392 |
|---|---|---|---|---|
| 1. | Less participation (<56.697 scores) | 10.92 | 13.89 | 11.74 |
| 2. | Moderate participation (56.697 to 73.135 scores) | 85.21 | 83.33 | 84.69 |
| 3. | More participation (>73.135 scores) | 3.87 | 2.78 | 3.57 |
|  | Total | 100.00 | 100.00 | 100.00 |
|  | Mean = 64.916 | SD = 8.219 | | |

The table 31 reveals that overall, majority of the respondents (84.69%) had moderate level of participation in the soil and water conservation programme, about ten per cent (11.74%) had less people's participation and hardly 3.57 per cent of them had higher participation.

The table further reveals the gender-wise picture. According to it, majority of the male respondents (85.21%) held moderate people's participation in the programme. Nearly ten per cent of them had less level of people's participation in the programme. Only a few of them (3.87%) had more people's participation in the soil and water conservation programme. Similarly, majority of the female respondents (83.33%) showed moderate level participation in the programme. More than ten per cent of them (13.89%) agreed to their less participation. Only a few of them (2.78%) had more people's participation in soil and water conservation programme. The figure 4 too reveals such a picture.

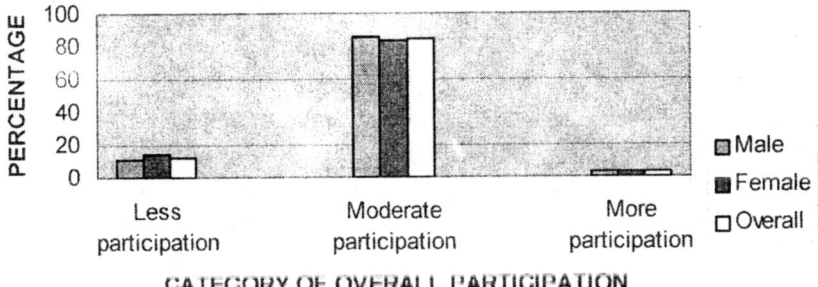

Fig. 4: Distribution of Respondents According to Overall People's Participation

## 3.7.7 PEOPLE'S PARTICIPATION IN PLANNING OF SOIL AND WATER CONSERVATION PROGRAMME

**People's participation levels in planning of the SWC programme:**

**Table 32: Percentage distribution of the respondents according to their participation levels in planning of the SWC programme.**

N=392

| Sr. No. | Participation levels | Respondent | | Overall (%) |
|---|---|---|---|---|
| | | Male (%) N=284 | Female (%) N=108 | N=392 |
| 1. | Less participation (<18.22 scores) | 11.27 | 13.89 | 11.99 |
| 2. | Moderate participation (18.22 to 25.27 scores) | 81.69 | 72.22 | 79.08 |
| 3. | More participation (>25.27 scores) | 7.04 | 13.89 | 8.93 |
| | Total | 100.00 | 100.00 | 100.00 |
| | Mean = 21.747 | SD = 3.524 | | |

Table 32 and figure 5 revealed that majority of the overall respondents (79.08%) exhibited moderate level of participation in the planning of the SWC programme. Then followed some little beyond ten per cent of them (11.99%) recorded less participation and less than ten per cent of them (8.93%) showed more participation level in planning of the soil and water conservation programme.

The table further shows that majority of the male respondents (81.69%) showed moderate level of participation, little more than ten per cent of them (11.27%) had less participation and hardly 7.04 per cent of them having more participation level in planning of the soil and water conservation programme. Whereas, on considering the female respondents participation, little less than three fourth of them (72.22%) had moderate level, little higher than ten per cent of them (13.89%) having less participation and also about the same percentage of them (13.89%) exhibited more participation in planning of the SWC programme.

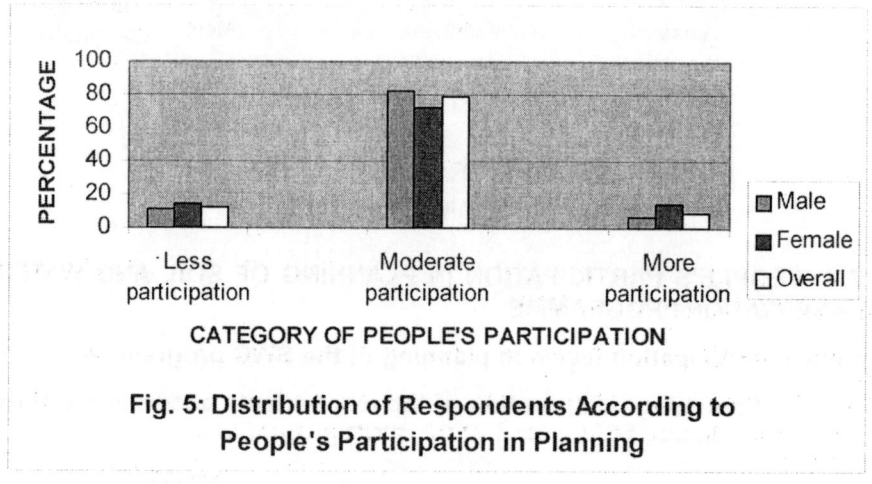

Fig. 5: Distribution of Respondents According to People's Participation in Planning

**Male's participation in the SWC programme planning stage:**

**Table 33: Itemwise percentage distribution and intensity indices according to the extent of male's participation in programme planning stage.**

N=284

| Sr. No. | Statements | GE% | SE% | LE/N% | Intensity indices |
|---|---|---|---|---|---|
| | **ITEMS** | | | | |
| 1. | Participate in planning meetings of Soil and Water Conservation (SWC) programme. | 76.05 | 18.31 | 5.64 | 2.70 |
| 2. | Suggest ideas during planning of checkdams. | 76.76 | 15.49 | 7.75 | 2.69 |

| 3. | Motivate fellow farmers to participate in planning. | 55.63 | 31.69 | 12.68 | 2.42 |
| 4. | Give suggestions for inclusion in planning. | 26.05 | 54.93 | 19.02 | 2.07 |
| 5. | Suggest ideas in planning of land levelling works. | 35.21 | 36.62 | 28.17 | 2.07 |
| 6. | Share experience about soil and water conservation with your fellow farmers after participation in planning meetings. | 32.39 | 42.96 | 24.65 | 2.07 |
| 7. | Suggest ideas in planning of agricultural crop cultivation. | 25.35 | 50.71 | 23.94 | 2.01 |
| 8. | Participate in planning of fruits plantation. | 17.60 | 66.20 | 16.20 | 2.01 |
| 9. | Suggest information in planning of forest trees plantation. | 33.80 | 31.69 | 34.51 | 1.99 |
| 10. | Contact the Programme Implementing Agency (PIA) about primary needs fuel, fodder and food to be taken care of in the planning. | 34.51 | 11.97 | 53.52 | 1.80 |

### The table 33 reveals that:

Fifty per cent or more of the male respondents participated to a great extent in the following activities related to the planning of the SWC programme:

- **Suggesting ideas during planning of checkdams (76.76%).**
- **Participating in planning meetings of the Soil and Water Conservation (SWC) programme (76.05%).**
- **Motivating fellow farmers to participate in planning (55.63%).**

Some fifty per cent or more of the male respondents participated in planning of SWC programme to some extent in the matters like:

- **Planning of fruits plantation (66.20%).**
- **Giving suggestions to be considered in planning (54.93%).**
- **Suggesting ideas in planning of agricultural crops cultivation (50.71%).**

Fifty per cent or more of the male respondents participated in planning of SWC programme to the least extent or never in matters like:

- **Contacting the Programme Implementing Agency (PIA) about primary needs fuel, fodder and food to be taken care of in the planning (53.52%).**

The table 33 further reveals that the intensity indices of people's participation in the programme and its planning, as the male respondents reported, ranged from 1.80 to 2.70. The male respondents showed high intensity indices in the following soil and water conservation programme planning activities:

- **Participating in planning meetings of the SWC programme (2.70).**
- **Suggesting idea in planning of checkdams in their fields (2.69).**

It further indicates that the male respondents participated highly in the SWC programme planning meetings and suggested ideas in planning of checkdams in their fields.

The male respondents showed moderate intensity indices in the following activities of planning of the soil and water conservation programme.

- **Motivating fellow farmers to participate in planning of SWC programme (2.42).**
- **Suggesting information to be considered in planning of the SWC programme (2.07).**
- **Suggesting ideas for planning of land levelling works carried out in the different fields of the watershed area (2.07).**
- **Share information or experience about soil and water conservation with their fellow farmers after participation in planning meetings (2.07).**
- **Participating in planning of fruits plantation work (2.01).**
- **Suggesting ideas in planning of agricultural crops cultivation in the watershed area (2.01).**
- **Suggesting information in planning of forest trees plantation work (1.99).**
- **Contacting the Programme Implementing Agency (PIA) about primary needs such as fuel, fodder and food to be taken care of in the programme planning (1.80).**

The table also indicates that the male respondents showed moderate participation in planning activities in the SWC programme. They did not show low level of participation in any planning activity of the soil and water conservation programme.

The extent of the people's participation in the programme planning stage, as explained by the male respondents was also analyzed with the developed people's participation index (PPI) and it was found to be 72.60 per cent, showing moderate level of participation in SWC technologies.

**Female's participation in the SWC programme planning stage:**

**Table 34: Itemwise percentage distribution and intensity indices according to the extent of female's participation in programme planning stage.**

N=108

| Sr. No. | Statements | GE% | SE% | LE/N% | Intensity indices |
|---|---|---|---|---|---|
| | **ITEMS** | | | | |
| 1. | Suggest idea during planning of checkdams. | 77.78 | 11.11 | 11.11 | 2.67 |
| 2. | Participate in planning meetings of Soil and Water Conservation (SWC) programme. | 61.11 | 30.56 | 8.33 | 2.53 |
| 3. | Suggest idea in planning of agricultural crops cultivation. | 36.12 | 44.44 | 19.44 | 2.16 |
| 4. | Share experience about soil and water conservation with fellow farmers after participation in planning meetings. | 44.44 | 25.00 | 30.56 | 2.13 |
| 5. | Give suggestion for inclusion in planning. | 25.00 | 61.11 | 13.89 | 2.11 |
| 6. | Motivate fellow farmers to participate in planning. | 36.11 | 38.89 | 25.00 | 2.11 |
| 7. | Contact the Programme Implementing Agency (PIA) about primary fuel, fodder and food to be taken care in the planning. | 44.44 | 16.67 | 38.89 | 2.05 |
| 8. | Suggest information in planning of forest trees plantation. | 30.56 | 38.89 | 30.55 | 2.00 |
| 9. | Participate in planning of fruits plantation. | 11.11 | 75.00 | 13.89 | 1.97 |
| 10. | Suggest idea in planning of land levelling works. | 22.22 | 36.11 | 41.67 | 1.80 |

**The table 34 reveals that:**

Fifty per cent or more of the female respondents participated in planning of the SWC programme to a great extent by -
- **Suggesting idea during planning of checkdams (70.78%).**
- **Participating in planning meetings of the Soil and Water Conservation (SWC) programme (61.11%).**

Fifty per cent or more of the female respondents participated in planning of the SWC programme to some extent in the matters like:
- **Planning of fruits plantation (75.00%).**
- **Giving suggestions to be considered in planning (61.11%).**

Forty per cent or more of the female respondents participated in planning of the SWC programme to the least extent or never in the matters like:
- **Suggesting idea in planning of land levelling works (41.67%).**

The table 34 further shows that the intensity indices of people's participation in programme planning stage as indicated by the female respondents ranged from 1.97 to 2.67. The female respondents showed high intensity index in the following planning activities of the soil and water conservation programme:
- **Suggesting idea during planning of checkdams in the watershed (2.67).**

It as well indicates that the female respondents contributed with high participation in the SWC programme and planning of checkdams in the watershed.

The female respondents showed moderate intensity indices of participation in the soil and water conservation programme and its planning activities listed below:
- **Participating in planning meetings of SWC programme (2.53).**
- **Suggesting idea in planning of agricultural crops cultivation in the watershed area (2.16).**
- **Share information or experience about soil and water conservation with their fellow farmers after participation in planning meetings (2.13).**
- **Suggesting information to be considered in planning of the SWC programme (2.11).**
- **Motivating their fellow farmers to participate in planning of SWC programme (2.11).**
- **Contacting the Programme Implementing Agency (PIA) about their primary needs such as fuel, fodder and food to be taken care of in the programme planning (2.05).**
- **Participating in suggestion of information in planning of forest tree plantation work (2.00).**
- **Participating in planning of various kinds of fruit plantation work (1.97).**

Suggesting idea during planning of land levelling works carried out in the different fields of the watershed area (1.80).

It means that the female respondents participated moderately in the SWC programme and its planning meeting by suggesting ideas in cultivation of crops, fruit plants and forestry plantation works etc.

They did not show low level of people's participation in any of the soil and water conservation programme and planning activity.

The female respondents' participation in programme planning stage was analyzed with the developed people's participation index (PPI) and it was found to be 72.03 per cent, showed moderate level of participation in SWC programme planning stage.

### 3.7.8 PEOPLE'S PARTICIPATION IN IMPLEMENTATION OF SWC PROGRAMME

People's participation levels in implementation of SWC programme:

Table 35: Distribution of the respondents according to their participation levels in implementation stage of SWC programme.

N=392

| Sr. No. | Participation levels In implementation | Respondent | | Overall (%) |
|---|---|---|---|---|
| | | Male (%) N=284 | Female (%) N=108 | N=392 |
| 1. | Less participation (<17.32 scores) | 20.78 | 16.67 | 19.64 |
| 2. | Moderate participation (17.32 to 24.53 scores) | 74.29 | 80.55 | 76.02 |
| 3. | More participation (>24.53 scores) | 4.93 | 2.78 | 4.34 |
| | Total | 100.00 | 100.00 | 100.00 |
| | Mean = 20.933 | SD = 3.604 | | |

The table 35 reveals that more than three fourth of the overall respondents (76.02%) showed moderate level of participation, nearly one fifth of them (19.64%) having less participation level and few of them with more participation level in implementation of the soil and water conservation programme.

However, the table 35 and figure 6 further indicates that nearly three fourth of the male respondents (74.29%) had moderate level of participation in implementation of the SWC programme. Then followed about one fifth of them (20.78%) with less participation level and about five per cent of them having higher participation in implementation of the soil and water conservation programme. Whereas, of the female respondents, the majority (80.55%) exhibited moderate level of participation in the implementation. They were followed by about fifteen per cent of them with less participation level and few of them having more participation level in implementation of the SWC programme.

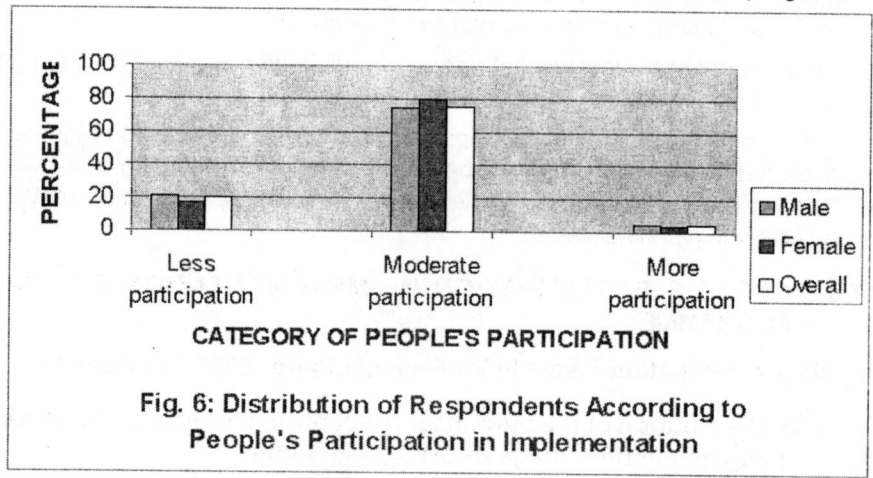

Fig. 6: Distribution of Respondents According to People's Participation in Implementation

**Male's participation in the SWC programme at the implementation stage:**

Table 36: Itemwise percentage distribution and intensity indices of the extent of male's participation in the SWC programme implementation stage.

N=284

| Sr. No. | Statements | GE% | SE% | LE/N% | Intensity indices |
|---|---|---|---|---|---|
| | **ITEMS** | | | | |
| 1. | Allow programme implementing agency (PIA) to implement soil and water conservation programme works. | 83.09 | 12.68 | 4.23 | 2.78 |
| 2. | Ask fellow resource users for labour and money contribution towards construction of structures. | 62.68 | 17.60 | 19.72 | 2.42 |
| 3. | Help during plantation work of fruit plants. | 36.62 | 39.44 | 43.94 | 2.12 |
| 4. | Help in plantation work of forest plants. | 40.14 | 31.69 | 28.17 | 2.11 |
| 5. | Provide any material to help construction of soil and water conservation structures. | 17.61 | 64.79 | 17.60 | 2.00 |

| | | | | | |
|---|---|---|---|---|---|
| 6. | Provide equipment to the PIA during construction of soil and water conservation measures. | 42.96 | 13.38 | 43.66 | 1.99 |
| 7. | Provide help during purchase of materials. | 35.21 | 28.17 | 36.62 | 1.98 |
| 8. | Contribute money in construction of SWC structures. | 33.10 | 28.87 | 38.03 | 1.95 |
| 9. | Contribute labour in construction of SWC structures. | 28.87 | 31.69 | 39.44 | 1.89 |
| 10. | Participate in training programme on the soil and water conservation programme organized by the PIA. | 7.75 | 65.49 | 26.76 | 1.80 |

**The table 36 reveals that:**

Fifty per cent or more of the male respondents participated in implementation of SWC programme to a great extent in the matters like:

- **Allowing programme implementing agency (PIA) to implement soil and water conservation programme works (83.09%).**
- **Asking fellow resource users to contribute with labour and money contribution towards construction of structures (62.68%).**

Fifty per cent or more of the male respondents participated in implementation of SWC programme to some extent in the matters like:

- **Participating in training on the soil and water conservation programme organized by the PIA (65.49%).**
- **Providing material to help construction of soil and water conservation structures (64.79%).**

Forty per cent or more of the male respondents participated in implementation of SWC programme to least or no extent in the matters like:

- **Helping during plantation work of fruit plants (43.94%).**
- **Providing equipment to the PIA during construction of soil and water conservation measures (43.66%).**

The table 36 further shows that the intensity indices of participation in the programme at the stage of implementation on the part of the male respondents ranged from 1.80 to 2.78. The male respondents showed high intensity index for the item:

- **Allowing programme implementing agency to implement SWC programme works (2.78).**

This indicates that the male respondents contributed to this activity of the SWC programme and its implementation with high level participation.

The male respondents showed moderate level of participation in the following activities of the soil and water conservation programme during implementation stage:

- Asking fellow resource users to contribute with labour and money towards construction of SWC structures (2.42).
- Helping during plantation work of fruit plants (2.12).
- Providing help in plantation work of forest plants (2.11).
- Providing material to help construction of SWC structures (2.00).
- Providing equipment during construction of SWC measures (1.99).
- Providing help during purchase of construction materials (1.98).
- Contributing with money in construction of SWC structures (1.95).
- Contributing with labour in construction of structures (1.89).
- Participating in training programme on the soil and water conservation technologies organized by PIA (1.80).

These findings indicate that the male respondents had moderate participation in the activities related to the SWC programme during implementation stage. They contributed material, labour and money in construction of structures, provided help during plantation works in watershed.

The extent of the male respondents' participation in the programme at the stage of its implementation was calculated also with the help of developed people's participation index (PPI) and it was found to be 69.29 per cent. It means that level of participation of male farmers in the implementation stage was moderate.

**Female farmers' participation in the SWC programme at the implementation stage:**

Table 37: Itemwise percentage distribution and intensity indices of the extent of female's participation in the SWC programme implementation stage.

N=108

| Sr. No. | Statements | GE% | SE% | LE/N% | Intensity indices |
|---|---|---|---|---|---|
| | **POSITIVE ITEMS** | | | | |
| 1. | Allow programme implementing agency (PIA) to implement soil and water conservation programme works. | 94.44 | 2.78 | 2.78 | 2.92 |
| 2. | Ask fellow resource users for labour and money contribution towards construction of structures. | 69.44 | 13.89 | 16.67 | 2.52 |

| | | | | | |
|---|---|---|---|---|---|
| 3. | Provide any material to help construction of soil and water conservation structures. | 30.56 | 61.11 | 8.33 | 2.22 |
| 4. | Contribute money in construction of SWC structures. | 38.89 | 36.11 | 25.00 | 2.13 |
| 5. | Provide equipment to the PIA during construction of soil and water conservation measures. | 41.67 | 25.00 | 33.33 | 2.08 |
| 6. | Provide help during purchase of materials. | 44.44 | 19.45 | 36.11 | 2.08 |
| 7. | Help in plantation work of forest plants. | 27.78 | 47.22 | 25.00 | 2.02 |
| 8. | Contribute labour to help construction of SWC structures. | 27.78 | 41.67 | 30.55 | 1.97 |
| 9. | Participate in training programmes on the soil and water conservation programme organized by PIA. | 11.11 | 72.22 | 16.67 | 1.94 |
| 10. | Help during plantation work of fruit plants. | 16.67 | 44.44 | 38.89 | 1.77 |

**The table 37 reveals that:**

Fifty per cent or more of the female respondents participated in implementation of the SWC programme to great extent in the matters like:

- **Allowing the programme implementing agency (PIA) to implement soil and water conservation programme works (94.44%).**
- **Asking fellow resource users to contribute with labour and money to construction of structures (69.44%).**

Fifty per cent or more of the female respondents participated in implementation of SWC programme to some extent in the matters like:

- **Participating in training programme on the soil and water conservation programme organized by the PIA (72.22%).**
- **Providing material to help construction of soil and water conservation structures (61.11%).**

Thirty five per cent or more of the male respondents participated in implementation of SWC programme to the least or no extent in the matters like:

- **Helping during plantation work of fruit plants (38.89%).**
- **Providing help during purchase of materials (36.11%).**

The table 37 further shows the intensity indices of participation in the programme at the stage of implementation on the part of the female respondents. It ranged from 1.77 to 2.92. They showed high intensity index in the following activity related to the soil and water conservation programme during implementation:

- **Allowed Programme Implementing Agency to implement SWC programme works (2.92).**

This indicates that the female respondents allowed PIA to implement conservation works on their fields in the SWC programme during implementation with considerably high participation.

The female respondents showed moderate intensity indices in the following activities of the soil and water conservation programme during implementaion:

- **Asking fellow resource users to contribute with labour and money to construction of SWC structures (2.52).**
- **Providing materials to help the construction of SWC structures (2.22).**
- **Contributing money in construction of SWC structures (2.13).**
- **Providing equipment to the Project Implementing Agency (PIA) during construction of SWC measures in watershed (2.08).**
- **Providing help during purchase of construction materials (2.08).**
- **Helping during plantation of forest plants (2.02).**
- **Contributing with labour to help construction of SWC structures (1.97).**
- **Participating in training programme on the soil and water conservation technologies organized by the PIA (1.94).**
- **Helping in plantation work of fruit plants (1.77).**

This indicates that the female respondents moderately participated in contribution of materials, labour and money in construction of structures and also provided help in plantation of fruits and forest plants during implementation stage of the SWC programme.

The extent of females' participation in the SWC programme implementation stage was calculated also with help of the developed people's participation index (PPI) and it was found to be 71.66 per cent. It reflects that female respondents' participation in implementation stage was moderate level.

## 3.7.9 PEOPLE'S PARTICIPATION IN MAINTENANCE OF THE SWC PROGRAMME

People's participation levels in the maintenance of the SWC programme:

Table 38: Distribution of the respondents according to their participation levels in maintenance of the SWC programme.

N=392

| Sr. No. | Participation levels In maintenance | Respondent Male (%) N=284 | Female (%) N=108 | Overall (%) N=392 |
|---|---|---|---|---|
| 1. | Less participation (<19.219 scores) | 11.62 | 12.04 | 11.74 |
| 2. | Moderate participation (19.219 to 25.231 scores) | 75.70 | 81.48 | 77.29 |
| 3. | More participation (>25.231 scores) | 12.68 | 6.48 | 10.97 |
| | Total | 100.00 | 100.00 | 100.00 |
| | Mean = 22.225 | | SD = 3.006 | |

It is seen from the table 38 and the figure 7 that little more than three fourth of the overall respondents (77.29%) showed moderate level of participation in the maintenance of the SWC programme. The remaining less than one fourth of them showed less and more participation level in maintenance of the soil and water conservation programme with 11.74 per cent and 10.97 per cent respectively.

The table 38 further shows that majority of the male farmers (75.70%) showed moderate level of participation, 12.68 per cent of them showed more participation level and some 11.62 per cent of them showed less participation in maintenance of the soil and water conservation programme. Further, majority of the female farmers (81.48%) had moderate level of participation, 12.04 per cent of them having less participation level and few of them having more participation level in maintenance stage of the SWC programme.

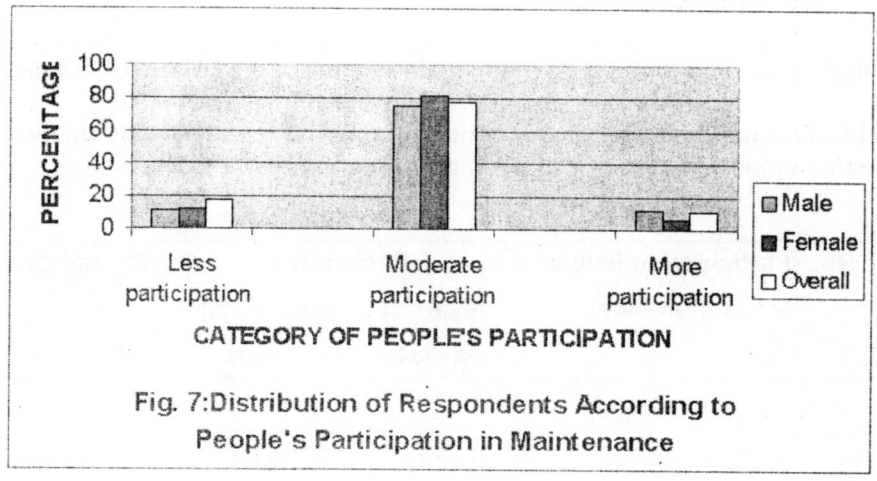

Fig. 7: Distribution of Respondents According to People's Participation in Maintenance

**Male's participation in the SWC programme at the maintenance stage:**

Table 39: Itemwise percentage distribution and intensity indices of the extent of male's participation in programme at the maintenance stage.

N=284

| Sr. No. | Statements | GE% | SE% | LE/N% | Intensity indices |
|---|---|---|---|---|---|
|  | **ITEMS** |  |  |  |  |
| 1. | Protect the forest plantation done in the watershed area. | 72.54 | 17.61 | 9.85 | 2.62 |
| 2. | Contribute money towards repair and maintenance of SWC structures. | 55.63 | 24.65 | 19.72 | 2.35 |
| 3. | Protect the SWC structures from natural calamities. | 41.55 | 38.73 | 19.72 | 2.21 |
| 4. | Inform the PIA officers to repair the damaged SWC structures. | 38.73 | 42.25 | 19.01 | 2.19 |
| 5. | Motivate fellow farmers for labour contribution towards repair and maintenance of SWC structures in the watershed. | 35.21 | 44.37 | 20.42 | 2.14 |

| | | | | | |
|---|---|---|---|---|---|
| 6. | Protect the fruit plants grown in the watershed area. | 23.24 | 65.49 | 11.27 | 2.11 |
| 7. | Motivate fellow farmers for money contribution towards repair and maintenance of SWC structures in the watershed. | 35.21 | 40.85 | 23.94 | 2.11 |
| 8. | Contribute own labour towards repair and maintenance of SWC structures. | 35.92 | 35.21 | 28.87 | 2.07 |
| 9. | Consult with the programme implementing agency to learn about repair and maintenance of conservation structures. | 37.32 | 27.46 | 35.21 | 2.02 |
| 10. | Take care of the forest and fruit plants during summer by providing irrigation. | 40.84 | 19.72 | 39.44 | 2.01 |

**The table 39 reveals that:**

Forty per cent or more male respondents participated in maintenance of the SWC programme to great extent in the activities like:

- **Protecting the forest plantation done in the watershed area (72.54%).**
- **Contributing with money towards repair and maintenance of SWC structures (55.63%).**
- **Protecting the SWC structures from natural calamities (41.55%).**
- **Take care of forest plants and fruit plants during summer by providing adequate irrigation (40.84%).**

Forty per cent or more male respondents participated in maintenance of the SWC programme to a some extent in the activities like:

- **Protecting fruit plants grown in the watershed area (65.49%).**
- **Motivating fellow farmers to extend contribution with labour to the repair and maintenance of SWC structures in the watershed (44.37%).**
- **Inform the PIA officers to repair the damaged SWC structures (42.25%).**
- **Motivating fellow farmers to extend contribution with their money to the repair and maintenance of SWC structures in the watershed (40.81%).**

Thirty five per cent or more male respondents participated in maintenance of the SWC programme to the least extent or never in the activities like:

- Taking care of forest plants and fruit plants during the summer by providing adequate irrigation (39.44%).
- Consulting the programme implementing agency to learn about repair and maintenance of conservation structures (35.21%).

The table 39 further shows the intensity indices of participation in programme maintenance stage by the male respondents. It ranged from 2.01 to 2.62. The male respondents showed high participation level in the following activity of the soil and water conservation programme maintenance stage:

- Protecting forest plantation done in the watershed area from animals (2.62).

The male respondents showed moderate participation level in the following activities of the soil and water conservation programme at the maintenance stage:

- Contributing with money towards repair and maintenance of SWC structure in their field (2.35).
- Protecting SWC structures from the natural calamities (2.21).
- Informing PIA officers to repair the damaged of SWC structures (2.19).
- Motivating fellow farmers to extend contribution with their labour to the repair and maintenance of SWC structures in the watershed (2.14).
- Protecting the fruit plants grown in the watershed area (2.11).
- Motivating fellow farmers to extend money contribution with their money to the repair and maintenance of SWC structures (2.11).
- Contributing with your labour to repair and maintenance of SWC structures in their field (2.07).
- Consulting the PIA to learn more about the repair and maintenance of conservation structures (2.02) and taken care of the forest and fruit plants during summer by providing irrigation (2.01).

It means male respondents moderately participated labour and money in repair and maintenance of structures in their fields and also protected plantations

The extent of male's participation in the SWC programme maintenance stage was also calculated with the help of the developed people's participation index (PPI) and it was calculated as 72.76 per cent. It shows that male farmers exhibited moderate level of participation during maintenance stage of SWC programme.

**Female's participation in the SWC programme at the maintenance stage:**

**Table 40: Itemwise percentage distribution and intensity indices of the extent of females' participation in the SWC programme at the maintenance stage.**

N=108

| Sr. No. | Statements | GE% | SE% | LE/N% | Intensity indices |
|---|---|---|---|---|---|
| | **ITEMS** | | | | |
| 1. | Protect the forest plantation done in the watershed area. | 77.78 | 11.11 | 11.11 | 2.66 |
| 2. | Contribute money towards repair and maintenance of SWC structures. | 44.44 | 38.89 | 16.67 | 2.37 |
| 3. | Contribute own labour towards repair and maintenance of SWC structures. | 55.56 | 22.22 | 22.22 | 2.36 |
| 4. | Protect the SWC structures from natural calamities. | 44.44 | 47.22 | 8.34 | 2.27 |
| 5. | Take care of the forest and fruit plants during summer by providing irrigation. | 55.00 | 22.22 | 27.78 | 2.22 |
| 6. | Motivate fellow farmers for money contribution towards repair and maintenance of SWC structures in the watershed. | 36.11 | 47.22 | 16.67 | 2.19 |
| 7. | Consult with the programme implementing agency to learn about repair and maintenance of conservation structures. | 38.89 | 33.33 | 27.78 | 2.11 |
| 8. | Protect the fruit plants grown in the watershed area. | 13.89 | 77.78 | 8.33 | 2.05 |
| 9. | Motivate fellow farmers for labour contribution towards repair and maintenance of SWC structures in the watershed. | 33.33 | 36.11 | 30.56 | 2.02 |
| 10. | Inform the PIA officers to repair the damaged SWC structures. | 22.22 | 52.78 | 25.00 | 1.97 |

The data of the table 40 reveal that:

Forty per cent or more female respondents participated in maintenance of the SWC programme to great extent in the activities like:

- **Protecting the forest plantation done in the watershed area (77.78%).**
- **Contributing with your own labour towards the repair and maintenance of SWC structures (55.56%).**
- **Taking care of forest plants and fruit plants during summer by providing irrigation (55.00%).**
- **Contributing money towards repair and maintenance of SWC structures.**
- **Protecting the SWC structures from natural calamities (44.44%).**

Forty per cent or more female respondents participated in maintenance of the SWC programme to some extent in the activities like:

- **Protecting fruit plants grown in the watershed area (77.78%).**
- **Informing the PIA officers to repair the damaged SWC structures (52.78%).**
- **Motivating fellow farmers to extend contribution with their money towards the repair and maintenance of SWC structures in the watershed (47.22%).**
- **Protecting the SWC structures from natural calamities (47.22%).**

Thirty per cent or more female respondents participated in maintenance of the SWC programme to the least extent or never in the activity like:

- **Motivating fellow farmers to extend contribution with their labour towards the repair and maintenance of SWC structures in the watershed (30.56%).**

The table 40 further shows the intensity indices for participation of female respondents in programme maintenance stage. It ranged from 1.97 to 2.66. The female respondents showed high participation level in the following activity of the soil and water conservation programme at the maintenance stage:

- **Protecting forest plantation done in the watershed area from animals (2.66).**

The female respondents showed moderate participation levels in the remaining following activities of the soil and water conservation programme at the maintenance stage:

- **Contributing money towards repair and maintenance of SWC structure in their field (2.37).**
- **Contributing labour towards the repair and maintenance of SWC structures in their field (2.33).**
- **Protecting SWC structures from the natural calamities (2.27).**
- **Taking care of forest plants and fruit plants during the summer season by providing adequate irrigation (2.22).**
- **Motivating fellow farmers to extend contribution with their money towards the repair and maintenance of SWC structures (2.11).**
- **Consulting the PIA to learn more about repair and maintenance of conservation structures (2.11).**
- **Protecting fruit plants grown in the watershed area (2.05).**
- **Motivating fellow farmers to extend contribution with their labour towards the repair and maintenance of SWC structures in the watershed (2.02).**
- **Informing the PIA officers to repair the damaged SWC structures (1.97).**

It shows that female respondents moderately participated labour and money in repair and maintenance of SWC structures were involved to take care of fruit and forestry plantation during summer season.

The female respondents did not show low level of people's participation in any activity of the soil and water conservation programme at the maintenance stage.

The extent of females' participation in the SWC programme maintenance stage was also calculated with the help of the developed people's participation index (PPI) and it was found to be 74.06 per cent. It shows moderate level of participation by female respondents in maintenance stage of soil and water conservation programme.

## 3.7.10 RELATIONSHIP BETWEEN INDEPENDENT VARIABLES AND DEPENDENT VARIABLES

Relationship between the male farmers' overall participation and the selected independent variables:

Table 41: Coefficient of correlation between the male farmers' overall participation in SWC programme and the selected independent variables.

N = 284

| Sr. No. | Independent Variables | Correlation Coefficient ('r' Values) |
|---|---|---|
| 1. | Age | 0.0629 |
| 2. | Socio-economic status | 0.293** |
| 3. | Land holding | 0.251** |
| 4. | Education | 0.176 |
| 5. | Farm power | 0.281** |
| 6. | Family size | 0.228* |
| 7. | Income | 0.047 |
| 8. | Social participation | 0.201* |
| 9. | Risk preference | 0.645** |
| 10. | Knowledge | 0.548** |
| 11. | Attitude | 0.593** |
| 12. | Adoption | 0.247* |

\* Significant at 5 per cent level of probability.
\*\* Significant at 1 per cent level of probability.

**Age and male farmers' overall participation:**

The table 41 reveals that age of the rural male farmers was positively and non-significantly correlated with their overall participation in the SWC programme with the correlation coefficient value at r=0.0629. It shows that the overall participation of the male farmers in the soil and water conservation programme increased non-significantly with the increase in their age.

Thus, the Null hypothesis (H1) that states that there will be no relationship between the age and the overall participation of male farmers in the SWC programme was accepted.

**Socio-economic status and male farmers' overall participation:**

The table 41 further shows that the socio-economic status of the rural male farmers was found to be positively and significantly correlated with the overall participation of the male farmers in the soil and water conservation programme with the correlation coefficient value at r=0.293. It is significant at 1 per cent level of probability. It shows that the level of overall participation of the rural male farmers increased significantly with increase in their socio-economic status.

Therefore, the Null hypothesis (H1) stating that there will be no significant relationship between the overall participation of male farmers in the SWC programme and the socio-economic status thus was not accepted.

### Land holding and male farmers' overall participation:

Regarding the land holding of rural male farmers the table observes that it was positively and significantly correlated with male farmers' overall participation in the soil and water conservation programme with the correlation coefficient value at r=0.251, at 1 per cent level of significance. It shows that as the size of the land holding increased the overall participation of male farmers also increased significantly.

Hence, the Null hypothesis (H1) stating that there will be no relationship between the land holding and the overall participation of male farmers in the SWC programme was not accepted.

### Education and male farmers' overall participation:

The table 41 shows that education among rural male farmers was positively and non-significantly correlated with their overall participation in the SWC programme with the correlation coefficient value at r=0.176. It shows that the level of overall participation of rural male farmers increased with the increase in their education level. It indicates that rural male farmers with high level of education participated more in planning, implementation and maintenance of the SWC programme, but it is non-significant.

The Null hypothesis (H1) that states that there will be no significant relationship between the overall participation of male farmers in the SWC programme and the level of education was accepted.

### Farm power and male farmers' overall participation:

The table 41 shows that the farm power of rural male farmers was observed positively and significantly correlated with their overall participation in the soil and water conservation programme with the correlation coefficient value r=0.281, Which is significant at 1 per cent level of probability. It shows that as the farm power increased the overall participation of male farmers in the soil and water conservation programme also increased.

Hence, the Null hypothesis (H1) stating that there will be no relationship between farm power and overall participation of male farmers in the SWC programme was not accepted.

### Family size and male farmers' overall participation:

The table 41 shows that family size of rural male farmers was found to be positively and significantly correlated with their overall participation in the soil and water conservation programme with the correlation coefficient value at $r=0.228$. This is significant at 1 per cent level of probability. It shows that the level of overall participation of male farmers increased with the increase in the size of their families.

The Null hypothesis (H1) stating that there will be no relationship between the family size and the overall participation of male farmers in the soil and water conservation programme was not accepted.

### Income and male farmers' overall participation:

In relation to the income of the rural male farmers the table indicates it was found positively and non-significantly correlated with the males' overall participation in soil and water conservation programme with the correlation coefficient value at $r=0.047$, which is non-significant. It shows that the level of overall participation of rural male farmers increased with the increase in their income, but it was non-significant.

The Null hypothesis (H1) stating that there will be no significant relationship between the overall participation of male farmers in the SWC programme and the income was accepted.

### Social participation and male farmers' overall participation:

It is seen from table 41 that social participation of rural male farmers was positively and significantly correlated with their overall participation in the soil and water conservation programme with the correlation coefficient value at $r=0.201$, which is significant at 5 per cent level of probability. It shows that the level of overall participation of male farmers increased with increase in their social participation.

The Null hypothesis (H1) stating that there will be no relationship between social participation and the overall participation of male farmers in the soil and water conservation programme was not accepted.

### Risk preference and male farmers' overall participation:

The table 41 also shows that there was high positive and significant correlation between the risk preference of rural male farmers and their overall participation in the soil and water conservation programme with the correlation coefficient value at $r=0.645$, which is significant at 1 per cent level of probability. It shows that the level of overall participation of male farmers increased with the increase in their risk preference in the soil and water conservation programme.

Thus, the Null hypothesis (H1) stating that there will be no relationship between the risk preference and overall participation of male farmers in the soil and water conservation programme was not accepted.

### Knowledge and male farmers' overall participation:

Table 41 shows that knowledge regarding the soil and water conservation technologies among male farmers was highly positively and significantly correlated with their overall participation in the soil and water conservation programme with the correlation coefficient value at r=0.548, which is significant at 1 per cent level of probability. It shows that the level of overall participation of male farmers increased with the increase in their knowledge regarding soil and water conservation technologies.

Thus, the Null hypothesis (H1) stating that there will be no relationship between the knowledge and overall participation of male farmers in the soil and water conservation programme was not accepted.

### Attitude and male farmers' overall participation:

The table 41 shows that the attitude of rural male farmers towards the soil and water conservation programme was also observed highly positively and significantly correlated with overall participation in the soil and water conservation programme with the correlation coefficient value at r=0.593, which is significant at 1 per cent level of probability. It shows that the level of overall participation of male farmers increased as their attitude towards the soil and water conservation programme grew more and more favourable.

Hence, the Null hypothesis (H1) stating that there will be no relationship between the kind of attitude and the overall participation of male farmers in the soil and water conservation programme was not accepted.

### Adoption and male farmers' overall participation:

The table indicates that the adoption behaviour of rural male farmers regarding soil and water conservation technologies was observed positively and significantly correlated with overall participation in the soil and water conservation programme with the correlation coefficient value at r=0.247, which is significant at 5 per cent level of probability. It shows that the level of overall participation of male farmers increased with the increase in their adoption level for soil and water conservation technologies.

Thus, the Null hypothesis (H1) stating that there will be no relationship between adoption and overall participation of male farmers in the soil and water conservation programme was not accepted.

**Relationship between the female farmers' overall participation and the selected independent variables:**

**Table 42: Coefficient of correlation between the female farmers' overall participation in the SWC programme and the selected independent variables.**

N = 108

| Sr. No. | Independent Variables | Correlation Coefficient ('r' Values) |
|---|---|---|
| 1. | Age | -0.195 |
| 2. | Socio-economic status | 0.226* |
| 3. | Land holding | 0.140 |
| 4. | Education | 0.227* |
| 5. | Farm power | 0.116 |
| 6. | Family size | 0.314** |
| 7. | Income | -0.276** |
| 8. | Social participation | 0.238* |
| 9. | Risk preference | 0.244* |
| 10. | Knowledge | 0.632** |
| 11. | Attitude | 0.310** |
| 12. | Adoption | 0.113 |

\* Significant at 5 per cent level of probability.
\** Significant at 1 per cent level of probability.

**Age and female farmers' overall participation:**

The data in the table 42 reveal that the age was negatively and non-significantly correlated with overall participation of female farmers in the soil and water conservation programme with the correlation coefficient value at r= -0.195. It shows that overall participation of the female farmers in the soil and water conservation programmes decreased with the increase in the age, but it was not significant.

Thus, the Null hypothesis (H2) stating that there will be no relationship between the age and the overall participation of female farmers in the soil and water conservation programme was accepted.

## Socio-economic status and female farmers' overall participation:

The table 42 further shows that the socio-economic status of the rural female farmers was found positively and significantly correlated with their overall participation in the soil and water conservation programme with the correlation coefficient value at r=0.226. It is significant at 5 per cent level of probability. It shows that the level of overall participation of the rural female farmers increased with the increase in their socio-economic status.

The Null hypothesis (H2) stating that there will be no significant relationship between the overall participation of female farmers in the soil and water conservation programme and the socio-economic status was not accepted.

## Land holding and female farmers' overall participation:

The table 42 shows that the land holding of rural female farmers was observed positively and non-significantly associated with females' participation in the soil and water conservation programme with the correlation coefficient value at r=0.140. It shows that as the size of the land holding increased the overall participation of female farmers also increased. In this case it is non-significant.

Hence, the Null hypothesis (H2) stating that there will be no relationship between the land holding and the overall participation of female farmers in the SWC programme was accepted.

## Education and female farmers' overall participation:

The table 42 also shows that education among rural female farmers was found positively and significantly correlated with their overall participation in the SWC programme with the correlation coefficient value at r=0.227, which is significant at 5 per cent level of probability. It shows that the level of overall participation of rural female farmers increased with the increase in level of education among them.

The Null hypothesis (H2) stating that there will be no significant relationship between the overall participation of female farmers in the SWC programme and the education was not accepted.

## Farm power and female farmers' overall participation:

The table 42 as well shows that the farm power of rural female farmers was observed positively and non-significantly correlated with their overall participation in the soil and water conservation programme with the correlation coefficient value at r=0.116. It shows that as the farm power increased the overall participation of female farmers in soil and water conservation programme also increased. But it is non-significant.

Hence, the Null hypothesis (H2) stating that there will be no relationship between the farm power and the overall participation of female farmers in the soil and water conservation programme was accepted.

**Family size and female farmers' overall participation:**

The table 42 further shows that the size of families of the rural female farmers was calculated positively and significantly correlated with females' overall participation in the soil and water conservation programme with the correlation coefficient value at r=0.314. This is significant at 1 per cent level of probability. It shows that the level of overall participation of womens increased with the increase in the size of their families.

The Null hypothesis (H2) stating that there will be no relationship between the family size and the overall participation of female farmers in the soil and water conservation programme was not accepted.

**Income and female farmers' overall participation:**

As the table 42 shows, the income of rural female farmers was found negatively and significantly correlated with the females' overall participation in the soil and water conservation programme with the correlation coefficient value at r=-0.276. It shows that the level of overall participation of rural female farmers decreased significantly with the increase in their income.

The Null hypothesis (H2) stating that there will be no significant relationship between the overall participation of female farmers in the SWC programme and the income was accepted.

**Social participation and female farmers' overall participation:**

The table 42 as well shows that social participation of rural female farmers was observed positively and significantly correlated with females' overall participation in the soil and water conservation programme with the correlation coefficient value at r=0.238, which is significant at 5 per cent level of probability. It shows that the level of overall participation of female farmers increased significantly with the increase in their social participation.

The Null hypothesis (H2) stating that there will be no relationship between the social participation and the overall participation of female farmers in the soil and waterconservation programme was not accepted.

**Risk preference and overall females' participation:**

The table 42 shows that the risk preference of rural female farmers was observed highly positively and significantly correlated with females' overall participation in the soil and water conservation programme with the correlation coefficient value at r=0.244, which is significant at 5 per cent level of probability. It shows that the level of overall participation of female farmers increased significantly with the increase in their risk preference in the soil and water conservation programme.

Thus, the Null hypothesis (H2) stating that there will be no relationship between the risk preference and the overall participation of female farmers in the soil and water conservation programme was not accepted.

### Knowledge and female farmers' overall participation:

The table 42 shows that knowledge regarding soil and water conservation technologies that the rural female farmers possessed was observed highly positively and significantly correlated with their overall participation in the soil and water conservation programme with the correlation coefficient value at r=0.632, which is significant at 1 per cent level of probability. It shows that the level of overall participation of female farmers increased with the increase in their knowledge regarding soil and water conservation technologies.

Thus, the Null hypothesis (H2) stating that there will be no relationship between the knowledge and overall participation of female farmers in the soil and water conservation programme was not accepted.

### Attitude and female farmers' overall participation:

The table 42 further shows that the attitude of rural female farmers towards the soil and water conservation programme was observed highly positively and significantly correlated with their overall participation in the soil and water conservation programme with correlation coefficient value at r=0.310, which is significant at 1 per cent level of probability. It shows that the level of overall participation of female farmers increased significantly as their favourable attitude towards the soil and water conservation programme grew more and more favourable.

Hence, the Null hypothesis (H2) stating that there will be no relationship between the attitude and overall participation of female farmers in the soil and water conservation programme was not accepted.

### Adoption and female farmers' overall participation:

The table 42 also shows that adoption behaviour of rural female farmers towards soil and water conservation technologies was observed positively and non-significantly correlated with their overall participation in the soil and water conservation programme with the correlation coefficient value at r=0.113. It shows that the level of overall participation of female farmers increased non-significantly with the increase in their adoption behaviour towards soil and water conservation technologies.

Thus, the Null hypothesis (H2) stating that there will be no relationship between the adoption behaviour and the overall participation of female farmers in the soil and water conservation programme was accepted.

**Relationship between the male farmers participation in the planning of the Soil and Water Conservation programme and the selected independent variables:**

**Table 43: Coefficient of correlation between the male farmers' participation in the planning of the SWC programme and the selected independent variables.**

N = 284

| Sr. No. | Independent Variables | Correlation Coefficient ('r' Values) |
|---|---|---|
| 1. | Age | 0.121 |
| 2. | Socio-economic status | 0.645** |
| 3. | Land holding | 0.219* |
| 4. | Education | -0.154 |
| 5. | Farm power | 0.253* |
| 6. | Family size | 0.181 |
| 7. | Income | 0.035 |
| 8. | Social participation | 0.278** |
| 9. | Risk preference | 0.568** |
| 10. | Knowledge | 0.402** |
| 11. | Attitude | 0.467** |
| 12. | Adoption | 0.177 |

\* Significant at 5 per cent level of probability.
\*\* Significant at 1 per cent level of probability.

**Age and male farmers participation in planning:**

The data presented in table 43 reveal that age was positively and non-significantly correlated with participation of male farmers in the planning of the soil and water conservation programme with correlation coefficient value at r=0.121. It shows that participation of male farmers in planning of soil and water conservation programmes increased with the increase in their age but it was non-significant.

Thus, the Null hypothesis (H3) stating that there will be no relationship between age and the participation of male farmers in the planning of the SWC programme was accepted.

### Socio-economic status and overall male farmers participation:

The table 43 also indicates that the socio-economic status of rural male farmers was found positively and highly significantly correlated with the males' participation in the planning of the soil and water conservation programme with the correlation coefficient value at $r=0.645$. It shows that the level of participation of rural male farmers in the planning increased significantly with the increase in their socio-economic status.

The Null hypothesis (H3) stating that there will be no significant relationship between the participation of male farmers in the planning of the SWC programme and the socio-economic status was not accepted.

### Land holding and male farmers' overall participation:

The table 43 also shows that the land holding of rural male farmers was observed positively and significantly associated with their participation in the planning of the soil and water conservation programme with the correlation coefficient value at $r=0.219$, which is significant at 5 per cent level of probability. It shows that the participation of male farmers in the planning increased with the increase in the size of their land holding.

Hence, the Null hypothesis (H3) stating that there will be no relationship between the land holding and the participation in the planning of the SWC programme was not accepted.

### Education and male farmers' participation in planning:

The table 43 also shows that the education among rural male farmers was found negatively and non-significantly correlated with their participation in the planning of the SWC programme with the correlation coefficient value at $r=-0.154$. It shows that the level of participation by rural male farmers in planning decreased with the increase in their education.

The Null hypothesis (H3) stating that there will be no significant relationship between the males' participation in the planning of the SWC programme and the education was accepted.

### Farm power and male farmers' participation in planning:

The table 43 also shows that the farm power of rural male farmers was observed positively and significantly associated with their participation in the planning of the soil and water conservation programme with the correlation coefficient value at $r=0.253$, which is significant at 5 per cent level of probability. It shows that as the farm power increased, the participation in the planning by male farmers also increased.

Therefore, the Null hypothesis (H3) stating that there will be no relationship between the farm power and the participation in the planning of the SWC programme was not accepted.

### The family size and male farmers' participation in planning:

The table 43 further shows that the size of families of rural male farmers was found positively and non-significantly correlated with their participation in planning of the soil and water conservation programme with the correlation coefficient value at r=0.181, which is non-significant. It shows that the participation in planning by rural male farmers increased with the increase in their size of families but it was at non-significant level.

The Null hypothesis (H3) stating that there will be no relationship between the family size and the male farmers' participation in planning of the soil and water conservation programme was accepted.

### Income and male farmers' participation in planning:

The table 43 also shows that the income of rural male farmers was calculated as positively and non-significantly correlated with the their participation in planning of the soil and water conservation programme with the correlation coefficient value at r=0.035. It shows that the level of participation by rural male farmers in planning increased slightly with the increase in their income but it is non-significant.

The Null hypothesis (H3) stating that there will be no significant relationship between the males' participation in planning of the SWC programme and their income was accepted.

### Social participation and males' participation in planning:

The table 43 shows that social participation of rural male farmers was observed highly positively and significantly correlated with their participation in planning of the soil and water conservation programme with the correlation coefficient value at r=0.278, which is significant at 1 per cent level of probability. It shows that the level of participation by male farmers in planning increased with the increase in their social participation.

Thus, the Null hypothesis (H3) stating that there will be no relationship between social participation and males' participation in planning of soil and water conservation programme was not accepted.

### Risk preference and male farmers' participation in planning:

The table 43 also shows that risk preference of rural male farmers was observed highly positively and significantly correlated with their participation in planning of the soil and water conservation programme with the correlation coefficient value at r=0.568, which is significant at 1 per cent level of probability. It shows that the level of participation by male farmers in planning increased with the increase in their risk preference towards the adoption of new improved soil and water conservation technologies.

Thus, the Null hypothesis (H3) stating that there will be no relationship between risk preference and males' participation in planning of the soil and water conservation programme was not accepted.

**Knowledge and male farmers' participation in planning:**

The table 43 as well shows that knowledge of rural male farmers regarding soil and water conservation technologies was observed highly positively and significantly correlated with their participation in planning of the soil and water conservation programme with the correlation coefficient value at $r=0.402$, which is significant at 1 per cent level of probability. It shows that the level of participation in planning by male farmers increased with the increase in their understanding and knowledge regarding soil and water conservation technologies.

Thus, the Null hypothesis (H3) stating that there will be no relationship between knowledge of male farmers and their participation in planning of the soil and water conservation programme was not accepted.

**Attitude and male farmers' participation in planning:**

The table 43 shows that the attitude of rural male farmers towards the soil and water conservation programme was also observed highly positively and significantly correlated with their participation in planning of the soil and water conservation programme with the correlation coefficient value at $r=0.467$, which is significant at 1 per cent level of probability. It shows that the level of participation in planning by male farmers increased as their attitude towards the soil and water conservation programme grew more and more favourable.

Hence, the Null hypothesis (H3) stating that there will be no relationship between males' participation in planning of the soil and water conservation programme and their attitude was not accepted.

**Adoption and male farmers' participation in planning:**

The table 43 further shows that the adoption behaviour of rural male farmers regarding soil and water conservation technologies was observed positively and non-significantly correlated with male farmers' participation in planning of the soil and water conservation programme with the correlation coefficient value at $r=0.177$, which is non-significant. It shows that the level of participation in planning by male farmers increased as their adoption behaviour regarding soil and water conservation technologies increased. But it is non-significant level.

Thus, the Null hypothesis (H3) stating that there wil be no relationship between male farmers' participation in planning of the soil and water conservation programme and their adoption behaviour was accepted.

**Relationship between the female farmers' participation in planning of the Soil and Water Conservation programme and the selected independent variables:**

**Table 44: Coefficient of correlation between the female farmers' participation in planning of the SWC programme and the selected independent variables.**

N = 108

| Sr. No. | Independent Variables | Correlation Coefficient ('r' Values) |
|---|---|---|
| 1. | Age | -0.110 |
| 2. | Socio-economic status | 0.680** |
| 3. | Land holding | -0.053 |
| 4. | Education | 0.063 |
| 5. | Farm power | 0.006 |
| 6. | Family size | 0.147 |
| 7. | Income | -0.417** |
| 8. | Social participation | 0.230* |
| 9. | Risk preference | 0.160 |
| 10. | Knowledge | 0.525** |
| 11. | Attitude | 0.273** |
| 12. | Adoption | 0.060 |

\* Significant at 5 per cent level of probability.
\*\* Significant at 1 per cent level of probability.

**Age and female farmers' participation in planning:**

The data presented in the table 44 reveal that the age was negatively and non-significantly correlated with participation of female farmers in planning of the soil and water conservation programme with the correlation coefficient value at r= -0.110. It shows that their participation in planning of the soil and water conservation programme decreased as their age increased. But, it was not upto the level of significant.

Thus, the Null hypothesis (H4) stating that there will be no relationship between female farmers' participation in planning of the soil and water conservation programme and their age was accepted.

**Socio-economic status and female farmers' participation in planning:**

The table 44 further shows that the socio-economic status of rural female farmers was computed as highly positively and significantly correlated with their participation in planning of the soil and water conservation programme with the correlation coefficient value at r=0.680. It was found significant at 1 per cent level of probability. It shows that the level of participation in planning by rural female farmers increased with the increase in their socio-economic status. It indicates that rural female farmers with high level of socio-economic status could have more participation in planning of the SWC programme.

The Null hypothesis (H4) stating that there will be no significant relationship between the female farmers' participation in planning of the soil and water conservation programme and their socio-economic status was not accepted.

## Land holding and female farmers' participation planning:

The table 44 also shows that the land holding of rural female farmers was observed slightly negatively and non-significantly correlated with their participation in planning of the soil and water conservation programme with the correlation coefficient value at r=-0.053. It shows that as the size of their land holding increased their participation in planning by female farmers decreased. But in this case it is non-significant.

Hence, the Null hypothesis (H4) stating that there will be no relationship between the female farmers' participation in planning of the SWC programme and their land holding was accepted.

## Education and female farmers' participation planning:

The table 44 shows that education among rural female farmers was found positively and non-significantly correlated with their participation in planning of the SWC programme with the correlation coefficient value at r=0.063. It shows that the level of participation in planning by rural female farmers increased with the increase in their education level, but it is non-significant.

The Null hypothesis (H4) stating that there will be no significant relationship between the females' participation in planning of SWC programme and the education among them was accepted.

## The farm power and female farmers' participation in planning:

The table 44 even shows that the farm power of rural female farmers was observed positively and non-significantly correlated with their participation in planning of the soil and water conservation programme with the correlation coefficient value at r=0.006. It shows that as the farm power owned by them increase the participation in planning by female farmers also increased. However, it is non-significant.

Hence, the Null hypothesis (H4) stating that there will be no relationship between female farmers' participation in planning of the soil and water conservation programme and their farm power was accepted.

### Family size and female farmers' participation in planning:

The table 44 also shows that the size of families of rural female farmers was calculated positively and non-significantly correlated with their participation in planning of the soil and water conservation programme with the correlation coefficient value at $r=0.147$. It shows that the level of women's participation in planning increased with the increase in the size of their families.

The Null hypothesis (H4) stating that there will be no relationship between the family size and female farmers' participation in planning of the soil and water conservation programme was accepted.

### Income and females' participation in planning:

The table 44 also shows that the income of rural female farmers was found negatively and significantly correlated with their participation in planning of the soil and water conservation programme with the correlation coefficient value at $r=-0.417$, which is significant at 1 per cent level of probability. It shows that the level of participation in planning by rural female farmers decreased with the increase in their income.

The Null hypothesis (H4) stating that there will be no significant relationship between the female farmers' participation in planning of the SWC programme and their income was not accepted.

### Social participation and female farmers' participation in planning:

The table 44 shows that social participation of rural female farmers was observed positively and significantly correlated with their participation in planning of the soil and water conservation programme with the correlation coefficient value at $r=0.230$, which is significant at 5 per cent level of probability. It shows that the level of participation in planning of female farmers increased with the increase in their social participation.

The Null hypothesis (H4) stating there will be no relationship between social participation and female farmers' participation in planning of the soil and water conservation programme was not accepted.

### Risk preference and female farmers' participation in planning:

The table 44 also shows that the risk preference of rural female farmers was observed positively and non-significantly correlated with their participation in planning of the soil and water conservation programme with the correlation coefficient value at $r=0.160$, which is non-significant. It shows that the level of female farmers' participation in planning increased with the increase in their risk preference in the soil and water conservation programme.

Thus, the Null hypothesis (H4) stating that there will be no relationship between the risk preference and female farmers' participation in planning of the soil and water conservation programme was accepted.

### Knowledge and female farmers' participation in planning:

The table 44 as well shows that knowledge of soil and water conservation technologies among rural female farmers was observed positively and highly significantly correlated with their participation in planning of the soil and water conservation programme with the correlation coefficient value at $r=0.525$, which is significant at 1 per cent level of probability. It shows that the level of participation in planning by female farmers increased with the increase in their knowledge about soil and water conservation technologies.

Thus, the Null hypothesis (H4) stating that there will be no relationship between female farmers' participation in planning of the soil and water conservation programme and their knowledge about it was not accepted.

### Attitude and female farmers' participation in planning:

The table 44 also shows that the attitude of rural female farmers towards the soil and water conservation programme was also observed positively and highly significantly correlated with their participation in planning of the soil and water conservation programme with the correlation coefficient value at $r=0.273$, which is significant at 1 per cent level of probability. It shows that the level of participation in planning by female farmers increased as their favourable attitude towards the soil and water conservation programme grew increasingly favourable.

Hence, the Null hypothesis (H4) stating that there will be no relationship between female farmers' participation in planning of the soil and water conservation programme and their attitude was not accepted.

### Adoption and female farmers' participation in planning:

The table 44 also shows that the adoption behaviour of rural female farmers towards soil and water conservation technologies was observed positively and non-significantly correlated with their participation in planning of the soil and water conservation programme with the correlation coefficient value at $r=0.060$. It shows that the level of participation in planning of female farmers increased with the increase in their adoption level towards soil and water conservation technologies. However, it is non-significant.

Thus, the Null hypothesis (H4) stating that there will be no relationship between female farmers' participation in planning of the soil and water conservation programme and their adoption behaviour was accepted.

**Relationship between the male farmers' participation in implementation of the SWC programme and the selected independent variables.**

**Table 45: Coefficient of correlation between the male farmers' participation in implementation of the SWC programme and the selected independent variables.**

N = 284

| Sr. No. | Independent Variables | Correlation Coefficient ('r' Values) |
|---|---|---|
| 1. | Age | -0.016 |
| 2. | Socio-economic status | 0.200* |
| 3. | Land holding | 0.090 |
| 4. | Education | -0.153 |
| 5. | Farm power | 0.211* |
| 6. | Family size | 0.182 |
| 7. | Income | 0.016 |
| 8. | Social participation | 0.120 |
| 9. | Risk preference | 0.538** |
| 10. | Knowledge | 0.579** |
| 11. | Attitude | 0.590** |
| 12. | Adoption | 0.190 |

\* **Significant at 5 per cent level of probability.**
\*\* **Significant at 1 per cent level of probability.**

**Age and male farmers' participation in the implementation:**

The data presented in the table 45 reveal that the age of male farmers was negatively and non-significantly correlated with their participation in implementation of the soil and water conservation programme with the correlation coefficient value at r= -0.016. It shows that participation of male farmers in implementation of the soil and water conservation programme decreased with the increase in their age, but it was non-significant.

Thus, the Null hypothesis (H5) stating that there will be no relationship between male farmers' participation in implementation of the SWC programme and their age was accepted.

## Socio-economic status and male farmers' participation in the implementation:

The table 45 further shows that the socio-economic status of rural male farmers was found positively and significantly correlated with their participation in implementation of the soil and water conservation programme with the correlation coefficient value at r=0.200. It is significant at 5 per cent level of probability. It shows that the level of participation in implementation by rural male farmers increased with the increase in their socio-economic status. It further indicates that rural male farmers with high level of socio-economic status could have more participation at the implementation stage by contribution of money or materials in the soil and water conservation programme on watershed basis.

The Null hypothesis (H5) stating that there will be no significant relationship between the male farmers' participation in implementation of the SWC programme and their socio-economic status was not accepted.

## Land holding and male farmers' participation in the implementation:

The table 45 further shows that the land holding of rural male farmers was observed positively and non-significantly associated with their participation in implementation of the soil and water conservation programme with the correlation coefficient value at r=0.090. It shows that as the size of their land holding increased the participation of male farmers in implementation of the soil and water conservation programme also increased.

Hence, the Null hypothesis (H5) stating that there will be no relationship between male farmers' participation in implementation of SWC programme and their land holding was accepted.

## Education and male farmers' participation in the implementation:

The table 45 as well shows that the education among rural male farmers was found negatively and non-significantly correlated with their participation in implementation of the SWC programme with the correlation coefficient value at r= -0.153. It shows that the level of participation in implementation by rural male farmers decreased with the increase in their education. It indicates that rural male farmers with high level of education had lower participation in implementation of the SWC programme, but it was non-significant.

The Null hypothesis (H5) stating that there will be no significant relationship between the male farmers' participation in implementation of the SWC programme and their education was accepted.

## Farm power and male farmers' participation in the implementation:

The table 45 also shows that the farm power of rural male farmers was observed positively and significantly associated with their participation in implementation of the soil and water conservation programme with the correlation coefficient value at r=0.211, which is significant at 5 per cent level of probability. It shows that as their farm power increased the participation in implementation by male farmers also increased.

Therefore, the Null hypothesis (H5) stating that there will be no relationship between the farm power and male farmers' participation in implementation of the SWC programme was not accepted.

### The family size and male farmers' participation in the implementation:

The table 45 even shows that the size of families of rural male farmers was found positively and non-significantly correlated with their participation in implementation of the soil and water conservation programme with the correlation coefficient value at r=0.182. It is non-significant. It shows that the participation in implementation by the male farmers increased with the increase in their size of family. However, it was at non-significant level.

The Null hypothesis (H5) stating that there will be no relationship between the family size and male farmers' participation in implementation of the soil and water conservation programme was accepted.

### Income and male farmers' participation in implementation:

The table 45 further shows that the income of rural male farmers was calculated as positively and non-significantly correlated with their participation in implementation of the soil and water conservation programme with the correlation coefficient value at r=0.016. It shows that the level of participation in implementation of the rural male farmers increased slightly with the increase in their income. It indicates that rural male farmers with more income have participated in implementation of the SWC programme. But it was at non-significant level.

The Null hypothesis (H5) stating that there will be no significant relationship between the male farmers participation in implementation of the SWC programme and their income was accepted.

### Social participation and male farmers' participation in the implementation:

The table 45 also shows that social participation of rural male farmers was observed positively and non-significantly correlated with their participation in implementation of the soil and water conservation programme with the correlation coefficient value at r=0.120. It shows that the level of participation of the male farmers' in the implementation increased with the increase in their social participation.

Thus, the Null hypothesis (H5) stating that there will be no relationship between social participation and male farmers' participation in implementation of the soil and water conservation programme was accepted.

### Risk preference and male farmers' participation in the implementation:

The table 45 even shows that the risk preference of rural male farmers was observed highly positively and significantly correlated with their participation in implementation of the soil and water conservation programme with the correlation coefficient value at r=0.538, which is significant at 1 per cent level of probability. It shows that the level of participation by the male farmers in the implementation increased with the increase in their risk preference in adoption of soil and water conservation technologies.

Thus, the Null hypothesis (H5) stating that there will be no relationship between the male farmers' participation in implementation of the soil and water conservation programme and their risk preference was not accepted.

### Knowledge and male farmers' participation in the implementation:

The table 45 further shows that the knowledge regarding soil and water conservation technologies among the male farmers was observed highly positively and significantly correlated with their participation in implementation of the soil and water conservation programme with the correlation coefficient value at r=0.579. It is significant at 1 per cent level of probability. This shows that the level of participation in implementation of the SWC programme by the male farmers increased with the increase in their knowledge regarding soil and water conservation technologies.

Thus, the Null hypothesis (H5) stating that there will be no relationship between male farmers' participation in implementation of the soil and water conservation programme and their knowledge was not accepted.

### Attitude and male farmers' participation in the implementation:

The table 45 also shows that attitude of rural male farmers towards the soil and water conservation programme was also observed highly positively and significantly correlated with their participation in implementation of the soil and water conservation programme with the correlation coefficient value at r=0.590, which is significant at 1 per cent level of probability. It shows that the level of participation by the male farmers in implementation of the SWC programme increased with the increase in their favourable attitude towards the soil and water conservation programme.

Hence, the Null hypothesis (H5) stating that there will be no relationship between male farmers participation in implementation of the soil and water conservation programme and their attitude was not accepted.

### Adoption behaviour and male farmers' participation in implementation:

The table 45 as well shows that the adoption behaviour of rural male farmers towards soil and water conservation technologies was observed positively and non-significantly correlated with their participation in implementation of the soil and water conservation programme with the correlation coefficient value at r=0.190, which is non-significant. It shows that the level of participation in implementation by the male farmers increased with the increase in their adoption level towards soil and water conservation technologies. But it was not upto significant level.

Thus, the Null hypothesis (H5) stating that there will be no relationship between male farmers' participation in implementation of the soil and water conservation programme and their adoption behaviour was accepted.

**Relationship between the female farmers' participation in implementation of the SWC programme and the selected independent variables:**

**Table 46: Coefficient of correlation between the female farmers' participation in implementation of the SWC programme and the selected independent variables.**

N = 108

| Sr. No. | Independent Variables | Correlation Coefficient ('r' Values) |
|---|---|---|
| 1. | Age | -0.240* |
| 2. | Socio-economic status | 0.302** |
| 3. | Land holding | 0.191 |
| 4. | Education | 0.346** |
| 5. | Farm power | 0.173 |
| 6. | Family size | 0.445** |
| 7. | Income | -0.258** |
| 8. | Social participation | 0.241* |
| 9. | Risk preference | 0.262** |
| 10. | Knowledge | 0.634** |
| 11. | Attitude | 0.322** |
| 12. | Adoption | 0.079 |

\*   Significant at 5 per cent level of probability.
\*\*  Significant at 1 per cent level of probability.

**Age and female farmers' participation in implementation:**

It is revealed from the table 46 that the age factor was found negatively and significantly correlated with participation by female farmers in implementation of the soil and water conservation programme with the correlation coefficient value at r=-0.240. It was found significant at 5 per cent level of probability. It shows that their participation in implementation of the soil and water conservation programme decreased with the increase in their age.

Thus, the Null hypothesis (H6) that states that there will be no relationship between females' participation in implementation of the soil and water conservation programme and their age was not accepted.

## Socio-economic status and female farmers' participation in the implementation:

The table 46 further shows that the socio-economic status of rural female farmers was computed as highly positively and significantly correlated with their participation in implementation of the soil and water conservation programme with the correlation coefficient value at $r=0.302$. It was found significant at 1 per cent level of probability. This shows that the level of participation in implementation by the rural female farmers increased with the increase in their socio-economic status. It indicates that rural female farmers with higher socio-economic status participated more effectively in implementation of the SWC programme through actual adoption of practices and by contributing equipment, materials, machinery and money.

The Null hypothesis (H6) stating that there will be no significant relationship between the female farmers' participation in implementation of the soil and water conservation programme and their socio-economic status was not accepted.

## Land holding and females' participation implementation:

The table 46 also shows that the land holding of rural female farmers was observed positively and non-significantly associated with their participation in implementation of the soil and water conservation programme with the correlation coefficient value at $r=0.191$. It shows that as the size of their land holding increased, their participation in the implementation also increased. But in this case it was non-significant.

Hence, the Null hypothesis (H6) stating that there will be no relationship between the land holding and female farmers' participation in implementation of the SWC programme was accepted.

## Education and female farmers' participation in the implementation:

The table 46 also shows that education among rural female farmers was found highly positively and significantly correlated with their participation in implementation of the SWC programme with the correlation coefficient value at $r=0.346$. It shows that the level of participation in the implementation by the rural female farmers increased with the increase in their education level.

The Null hypothesis (H6) stating that there will be no significant relationship between the female farmers' participation in implementation of the SWC programme and their education was not accepted.

## Farm power and female farmers' participation in the implementation:

The table 46 further shows that the farm power owned by rural female farmers was observed positively and non-significantly associated with their participation in implementation of the soil and water conservation programme with the correlation coefficient value at r=0.173. It shows that as the farm power increased the participation in implementation of the SWC programme by the female farmers also increased. However, it was non-significant.

Hence, the Null hypothesis (H6) stating that there will be no relationship between the farm power and female farmers' participation in implementation of the soil and water conservation programme was accepted.

**The family size and female farmers' participation in the implementation:**

The table 46 as well shows that the size of the families rural female farmers was calculated positively and highly significantly correlated with their participation in implementation of the soil and water conservation programme with the correlation coefficient value at r=0.445. It is significant at 1 per cent level of probability. It shows that the level of women's participation in implementation of the SWC programme increased with the increase in the size of their families.

The Null hypothesis (H6) stating that there will be no relationship between the family size and female farmers' participation in implementation of the soil and water conservation programme was not accepted.

**Income and female farmers' participation in planning:**

The table 46 further shows that the income raised by rural female farmers was found negatively and highly significantly correlated with their participation in implementation of the soil and water conservation programme with the correlation coefficient value at r=-0.258. It is significant at 1 per cent level of probability. This shows that the level of participation in implementation of the SWC programme by the rural female farmers decreased with the increase in their income.

The Null hypothesis (H6) stating that there will be no significant relationship between the female farmers' participation in implementation of the SWC programme and their income was not accepted.

**Social participation and female farmers' participation in the implementation:**

The table 46 also shows that the social participation of rural female farmers was observed positively and significantly correlated with their participation in implementation of the soil and water conservation programme with the correlation coefficient value at r=0.241. It is significant at 5 per cent level of probability. This shows that the level of participation by the female farmers in implementation of the SWC programme increased with the increase in their social participation.

The Null hypothesis (H6) stating that there will be no relationship between female farmers' participation in implementation of the soil and water conservation programme and their social participation was not accepted.

### Risk preference and female farmers' participation in the implementation:

The table 46 further shows that the risk preference of rural female farmers was observed positively and highly significantly correlated with their participation in implementation of the soil and water conservation programme with the correlation coefficient value at r=0.262. It is significant at 1 per cent level of probability. This shows that the level of participation in implementation by the female farmers increased with the increase in their risk preference in adoption of soil and water conservation measures. It might be due to this fact that the higher risk preferred rural female farmers were oriented towards maximization of income from agriculture by adopting different soil and water conservation structures on their land.

Thus, the Null hypothesis (H6) stating that there will be no relationship between female farmers' participation in implementation of the soil and water conservation programme and their risk preference was not accepted.

### Knowledge and female farmers' participation in the implementation:

The table 46 also shows that knowledge level among rural female farmers regarding soil and water conservation technologies was observed positively and highly significantly correlated with their participation in implementation of the soil and water conservation programme with the correlation coefficient value at r=0.634. This is significant at 1 per cent level of probability. It shows that the level of participation in the implementation by the female farmers increased with the increase in their knowledge regarding soil and water conservation technologies.

Thus, the Null hypothesis (H6) stating that there will be no relationship between knowledge and female farmers' participation in implementation of the soil and water conservation programme their knowledge about it was not accepted.

### Attitude and female farmers' participation in the implementation:

The table 46 as well shows that attitude of rural female farmers towards the soil and water conservation programme was also observed positive and highly significantly correlated with their participation in implementation of the soil and water conservation programme with the correlation coefficient value at r=0.322. It is significant at 1 per cent level of probability. It shows that the level of participation in implementation by the female farmers increased as their favourable attitude towards soil and water conservation programme grew more and more favourable.

Hence, the Null hypothesis (H6) stating that there will be no relationship between females' participation in implementation of soil and water conservation programme and their attitude was not accepted.

### Adoption and female farmers' participation in the implementation:

The table 46 further shows that the adoption behaviour of rural female farmers towards soil and water conservation technologies was observed positive and non-significantly correlated with their participation in implementation of the soil and water conservation programme with the correlation coefficient value at r=0.079. It shows that the level of participation in the implementation by the female farmers increased with the increase in their adoption level towards soil and water conservation technologies. However, it was at non-significant level.

Thus, the Null hypothesis (H6) stating that there will be no relationship between female farmers' participation in implementation of the soil and water conservation programme and their adoption behaviour was accepted.

### Relationship between the male farmers' participation in maintenance of the SWC programme and the selected independent variables:

**Table 47: Coefficient of correlation between the male farmers' participation in maintenance of the SWC programme and the selected independent variables.**

N = 284

| Sr. No. | Independent Variables | Correlation Coefficient ('r' Values) |
|---|---|---|
| 1. | Age | 0.056 |
| 2. | Socio-economic status | 0.341** |
| 3. | Land holding | 0.317** |
| 4. | Education | -0.159 |
| 5. | Farm power | 0.271** |
| 6. | Family size | 0.240* |
| 7. | Income | 0.067 |
| 8. | Social participation | 0.107 |
| 9. | Risk preference | 0.586** |
| 10. | Knowledge | 0.472** |
| 11. | Attitude | 0.510** |
| 12. | Adoption | 0.376** |

\*   Significant at 5 per cent level of probability.
\*\*  Significant at 1 per cent level of probability.

### Age and male farmers' participation in maintenance:

The data presented in the table 47 reveal that the age was positively and non-significantly correlated with male farmers' participation in maintenance of the soil and water conservation programme with the correlation coefficient value at $r=0.056$. It shows that participation of the male farmers in maintenance of soil and water conservation structures on their farm increased with the increase in their age. But it was non-significant.

Thus, the Null hypothesis (H7) stating that there will be no relationship between males' participation in maintenance of the SWC programme and their age was accepted.

### The socio-economic status and male farmers' participation in maintenance:

The table 47 further shows that the socio-economic status of rural male farmers was found positively and significantly correlated with their participation in maintenance of the soil and water conservation programme with the correlation coefficient value at $r=0.341$. It is significant at 1 per cent level of probability. It shows that the level of participation in the maintenance by the rural male farmers increased with the increase in their socio-economic status.

The Null hypothesis (H7) stating that there will be no significant relationship between the male farmers' participation in maintenance of the SWC programme and their socio-economic status was not accepted.

### The land holding and male farmers' participation in the maintenance:

The table 47 also shows that the land holding of rural male farmers was observed positively and highly significantly associated with their participation in maintenance of the soil and water conservation programme with the correlation coefficient value at $r=0.317$. It is significant at 1 per cent level of probability. It shows that as the size of the land holding increased, the participation by the male farmers in maintenance of SWC measures also increased.

Hence, the Null hypothesis (H7) stating that there will be no relationship between male farmers' participation in maintenance of SWC programme and their land holding was not accepted.

### Education and male farmers' participation in the implementation maintenance:

The table 47 also shows that education among rural male farmers was found negatively and non-significantly correlated with their participation in maintenance of the SWC programme with the correlation coefficient value at $r=-0.159$. It shows that the level of participation in the maintenance by rural male farmers decreased as the level of education among them enhanced. It indicates that rural male farmers with high level of education imparted less labour as contribution to the repair and maintenance of SWC structures on their land. But it was non-significant.

The Null hypothesis (H7) stating there will be no significant relationship between the male farmers' participation in maintenance of SWC technologies and their education was accepted.

### The farm power and male farmers' participation in maintenance:

The table 47 further shows that the farm power owned be rural male farmers was observed positively and significantly associated with their participation in maintenance of the soil and water conservation programme with the correlation coefficient value at r=0.271. It is significant at 1 per cent level of probability. It indicates that as their farm power ownership increase, their participation in the repair and maintenance of soil and water conservation structures also increased.

Therefore, the Null hypothesis (H7) stating that there will be no relationship between male farmers' participation in maintenance of SWC programme the farm power owned by them was not accepted.

### The family size and male farmers' participation in the maintenance:

The table 47 shows that the size of families of rural male farmers was found positively and significantly correlated with their participation in maintenance of the soil and water conservation programme with the correlation coefficient value at r=0.240. It is significant at 5 per cent level of probability. This shows that the participation by the male farmers in maintenance of the SWC programme increased with the increase in the size of their families.

The Null hypothesis (H7) stating that there will be no relationship between the family size and male farmers' participation in maintenance of the soil and water conservation programme was not accepted.

### Income and male farmers' participation in the maintenance:

The table 47 also shows that the income raised by rural male farmers was calculated as positively and non-significantly correlated with their participation in maintenance of the soil and water conservation programme with the correlation coefficient value at r=0.067. It shows that the level of participation by the rural male farmers at the maintenance stage of the SWC programme increased slightly with the increase in their income. It indicates that as the rural male farmers got more income they could have more participation in maintenance of the SWC programme. But it was at non-significant level.

The Null hypothesis (H7) stating that there will be no significant relationship between the male farmers' participation in maintenance of SWC programme and their income was accepted.

### The social participation and male farmers' participation in the maintenance:

The table 47 further shows that the social participation of the rural male farmers was observed positively and non-significantly correlated with their participation in maintenance of the soil and water conservation programme with the correlation coefficient value at r=0.107. It is non-significant. This shows that the level of participation in maintenance by the male farmers increased with the increase in their social participation. It, however, remained at non-significant level.

Thus, the Null hypothesis (H7) stating that there will be no relationship between male farmers' participation in maintenance of the soil and water conservation programme and their social participation was accepted.

### Risk preference and male farmers' participation in the maintenance:

The table 47 as well shows that the risk preference of the rural male farmers was observed positively and highly significantly correlated with their participation in maintenance of the soil and water conservation programme with the correlation coefficient value at r=0.586. It is highly significant at 1 per cent level of probability. This indicates that the level of participation in the repair and maintenance of soil and water conservation structures by the male farmers increased with the increase in their risk preference towards adoption of new SWC technologies.

Thus, the Null hypothesis (H7) stating that there will be no relationship between the risk preference and male farmers' participation in maintenance of the soil and water conservation programme was not accepted.

### Knowledge and male farmers' participation in the maintenance:

The table 47 also shows that knowledge regarding soil and water conservation technologies among the rural male farmers was observed positively and highly significantly correlated with their participation in maintenance of the soil and water conservation programme with the correlation coefficient value at r=0.472. It is highly significant at 1 per cent level of probability. This shows that the level of participation in the maintenance by the male farmers increased with the increase in their knowledge regarding new soil and water conservation technologies.

Thus, the Null hypothesis (H7) stating that there will be no relationship between knowledge and male farmers' participation in maintenance of soil and water conservation programme was not accepted.

### Attitude and male farmers' participation in the maintenance:

The table 47 further shows that the attitude of the rural male farmers towards the soil and water conservation programme was observed positively and highly significantly correlated with their participation in maintenance of the soil and water conservation programme with the correlation coefficient value at r=0.510. It is significant at 1 per cent level of probability. This shows that the level of participation in the maintenance by the male farmers increased as their attitude towards soil and water conservation programme grew favourable.

Hence, the Null hypothesis (H7) stating that there will be no relationship between male farmers' participation in maintenance of the soil and water conservation programme was not accepted.

**Adoption and male farmers' participation in the maintenance:**

The table 47 as well that the adoption level of the rural male farmers towards soil and water conservation technologies was observed positively and highly significantly correlated with their participation at the maintenance stage of the soil and water conservation programme with the correlation coefficient value at r=0.376. It is significant at 1 per cent level of probability. This shows that the level of participation in the maintenance by the male farmers increased with the increase in their adoption behaviour towards soil and water conservation technologies.

Thus, the Null hypothesis (H7) stating that there will be no relationship between male farmers' participation in maintenance of the soil and water conservation programme and their adoption was accepted.

**Relationship between the female farmers' participation in maintenance of the SWC programme and the selected independent variables.**

**Table 48: Coefficient of correlation between the female farmers' participation in maintenance of the SWC programme and the selected independent variables.**

N = 108

| Sr. No. | Independent Variables | Correlation Coefficient ('r' Values) |
|---|---|---|
| 1. | Age | -0.190 |
| 2. | Socio-economic status | 0.276** |
| 3. | Land holding | 0.293** |
| 4. | Education | 0.240* |
| 5. | Farm power | 0.161 |
| 6. | Family size | 0.287** |
| 7. | Income | -0.016 |
| 8. | Social participation | 0.164 |
| 9. | Risk preference | 0.250* |
| 10. | Knowledge | 0.553** |
| 11. | Attitude | 0.239* |
| 12. | Adoption | 0.336** |

\* Significant at 5 per cent level of probability.
\*\* Significant at 1 per cent level of probability.

## Age and females' participation in maintenance:

It is revealed from the table 48 that the age was found negatively and non-significantly correlated with participation by the female farmers in maintenance of the soil and water conservation programme with the correlation coefficient value at r= -0.190. It is non-significant. This shows that participation by the female farmers in maintenance of the soil and water conservation programme decreased with the increase in their age. However, it was at non-significant level.

Thus, the Null hypothesis (H8) stating that there will be no relationship between female farmers' participation in maintenance of the soil and water conservation programme and their age was not accepted.

## The socio-economic status and female farmers' participation in maintenance:

The table 48 also indicates that the socio-economic status of the rural female farmers was computed as positively and significantly correlated with their participation in maintenance of the soil and water conservation programme with the correlation coefficient value at r=0.276. It was found significant at 1 per cent level of probability. This shows that the level of participation in maintenance by the rural female farmers increased with the increase in their socio-economic status.

The Null hypothesis (H8) stating that there will be no significant relationship between the male farmers' participation in maintenance of the soil and water conservation programme and their socio-economic status was not accepted.

## The land holding and females' participation in the maintenance:

The table 48 further shows that the land holding of the rural female farmers was observed positively and significantly associated with their participation in maintenance of the soil and water conservation programme with the correlation coefficient value at r= 0.293. It is significant at 1 per cent level of probability. This shows that as the size of land holding increased, the participation by the female farmers at the maintenance stage of SWC programme decreased.

Hence, the Null hypothesis (H8) stating that there will be no significant relationship between the land holding and female farmers' participation in maintenance of the SWC programme was not accepted.

## Education and female farmers' participation in maintenance:

The table 48 further shows that education among the rural female farmers was computed as positively and significantly correlated with their participation in maintenance of the SWC programme with the correlation coefficient value at r=0.240. It is significant at 5 per cent level of probability. This indicates that the level of participation at the maintenance stage by the rural female farmers increased with the increase in the level of education among them.

The Null hypothesis (H8) stating that there will be no significant relationship between the female farmers' participation in maintenance of the SWC programme and their education was not accepted.

**The farm power and female farmers' participation in the maintenance:**

The table 48 also shows that the farm power owned by the rural female farmers was observed positively and non-significantly associated with their participation in maintenance of the soil and water conservation programme with the correlation coefficient value at r=0.161. It is non-significant. This shows that as the farm power increased the participation at the maintenance stage of the SWC programme by the female farmers also increased. It, however, was at non-significant level.

Hence, the Null hypothesis (H8) stating that there will be no significant relationship between the female farmers' participation in maintenance of the soil and water conservation programme and the farm power owned by them was accepted.

**The family size and female farmers' participation in the maintenance:**

The table 48 as well shows that the size of families of the rural female farmers was calculated as positively and highly significantly correlated with their participation in maintenance of the soil and water conservation programme with the correlation coefficient value at r=0.287. It shows that the level of women's participation in maintenance of the soil and water conservation programme increased with the increase in the size of their families.

The Null hypothesis (H8) stating that there will be no significant relationship between the family size and female farmers' participation in maintenance of the soil and water conservation programme was not accepted.

**Income and female farmers' participation in maintenance:**

The table 48 further indicates that the income raised by the rural female farmers was found negatively and non-significantly correlated with their participation in maintenance of the soil and water conservation programme with the correlation coefficient value at r=-0.016. It is non-significant. This shows that the level of participation in maintenance by the rural female farmers decreased with the increase in their income. But it remained at non-significant level.

The Null hypothesis (H8) stating that there will be no significant relationship between the female farmers' participation in maintenance of the SWC programme and their income was accepted.

**The social participation and female farmers' participation in the maintenance:**

The table 48 as well shows that the social participation of the rural female farmers was observed positively and non-significantly correlated with their participation in maintenance of the soil and water conservation programme with the correlation coefficient value at r=0.164. It is non-significant. This shows that the level of participation by the female farmers in maintenance of the SWC programme increased with the increase in their social participation. But it was at non-significant level.

The Null hypothesis (H8) stating that there will be no significant relationship between female farmers' participation in maintenance of the soil and water conservation programme and social participation was accepted.

### The risk preference and female farmers' participation in the maintenance:

The table 48 further shows that the risk preference of the rural female farmers was observed positively and significantly correlated with their participation in maintenance of the soil and water conservation programme with the correlation coefficient value at r=0.250. It is significant at 5 per cent level of probability. This shows that the level of participation by the female farmers at the maintenance stage increased with the increase in their risk preference in adoption of soil and water conservation measures.

Thus, the Null hypothesis (H8) stating that there will be no significant relationship between the risk preference and female farmers' participation in maintenance of the soil and water conservation programme was not accepted.

### Knowledge and female farmers' participation in the maintenance:

The table 48 as well shows that the knowledge regarding soil and water conservation technologies among the rural female farmers was observed positively and highly significantly correlated with their participation in maintenance of the soil and water conservation programme with the correlation coefficient value at r=0.553. It is significant at 1 per cent level of probability. This shows that the level of participation in maintenance by the female farmers increased with the increase in their knowledge regarding soil and water conservation technologies.

Thus, the Null hypothesis (H8) stating that there will be no significant relationship between female farmers' participation in maintenance of the soil and water conservation programme and their knowledge was not accepted.

### Attitude and female farmers' participation in the maintenance:

The table 48 further shows that the attitude of the rural female farmers towards the soil and water conservation programme was computed as positively and significantly correlated with their participation in maintenance of the soil and water conservation programme with the correlation coefficient value at r=0.239. It is significant at 5 per cent level of probability. This shows that the level of participation in maintenance by the female farmers increased as their favourable attitude towards soil and water conservation programme grew increasingly favourable.

Hence, the Null hypothesis (H8) stating that there will be no significant relationship between females' participation in maintenance of the soil and water conservation programme their attitude was not accepted.

**Adoption and female farmers' participation in the maintenance:**

The table 48 as well shows that the adoption behaviour of the rural female farmers towards soil and water conservation technologies was observed positively and highly significantly correlated with their participation in maintenance of the soil and water conservation programme with the correlation coefficient value at r=0.336. It is significant at 1 per cent level of probability. This shows that the level of participation in maintenance of soil and water conservation structures by the female farmers increased with the increase in their adoption of soil and water conservation technologies.

Thus, the Null hypothesis (H8) stating that there will be no relationship between female farmers' participation in maintenance of the soil and water conservation programme and their adoption behaviour was not accepted.

**Relationship between the dependent variables of people's participation in the SWC programme and the independent variabe gender.**

**Table 49: Coefficient of correlation between the dependent variables of people's participation in SWC programme and the independent variabe gender.**

N = 392

| Sr. No. | Dependent Variables Dependent | Mean score values Male | Mean score values Female | Correlation Coefficient ('r' Values) |
|---|---|---|---|---|
| 1. | People's overall participation | 64.81 | 65.33 | -0.025 |
| 2. | People's participation in planning | 21.78 | 21.61 | 0.019 |
| 3. | People's participation in implementation | 20.79 | 21.50 | -0.078 |
| 4. | People's participation in maintenance | 21.82 | 22.22 | 0.003 |

**Gender and overall people's participation:**

The data regarding point biserial correlation are presented in table 49 above. The point biserial correlation was used to compute correlation between continuous variables of people's participation in different stages and the two-categorized or dichotomous variable i.. gender. It is revealed from the table that the gender was negatively and non-significantly correlated with people's overall participation in the soil and water conservation programme with the point biserial correlation value at r=-0.025, which is non-significant. This shows that no difference was noticed in people's overall participation in the soil and water conservation programme as an effect of the male and female categories of the respondents.

Hence, the Null hypothesis that stating that there will be no significant relationship between people's overall participation in the soil and water conservation programme and their gender was accepte.

### Gender and people's participation in the planning:

Gender was found positively and non-significantly correlated with people's participation in planning of the soil and water conservation programme with the point biserial correlation value at r=0.019. It is non-significant. This shows that no difference was noticed in people's participation in planning of the soil and water conservation programme based on the male and female categories of the respondents.

Hence, the Null hypothesis that stating that there will be no significant relationship between people's participation in planning of the soil and water conservation programme and their gender was accepte.

### Gender and people's participation in the implementation:

It is also revealed from the table that the gender was negatively and non-significantly correlated with people's participation in implementation of the soil and water conservation programme with the point biserial correlation value at r=-0.078. It is non-significant. This shows that no difference was noticed in people's participation in the implementation stage of the soil and water conservation programme among the respondents due to the gender differences.

Hence, the Null hypothesis that stating that there will be no significant relationship between people's participation in implementation of the soil and water conservation programme and their gender was accepted.

### Gender and people's participation in the maintenance:

It was as well found that the gender was positively and non-significantly correlated with people's participation in maintenance of the soil and water conservation programme with the point biserial correlation value at r=0.003. This shows that no difference was noticed in people's participation in the maintenance stage of the soil and water conservation programme due to the gender differences.

Hence, the Null hypothesis that stating that there will be no significant relationship between people's participation at the maintenance stage of the soil and water conservation programme and their gender was accepted.

It gets revealed from the table 49 that the gender does not have significant correlation with different dependent variables of people's participation in the SWC programme. Therefore, it may be concluded that there is no significant difference between the participation of the male respondents and the female respondents in the extent of people's overall participation and as well in the different stages of the Antisar watershed development programme, such as planning, implementation and maintenance. Thus, the female respondents are said to be as equal as male respondents in their interest, involvement and participation of the SWC programme.

### 3.7.11 CONSTRAINTS FACED BY RESPONDENTS

**Constraints faced by the male respondents:**

**Table 50: Itemwise percentage distribution and rank order of the constraints faced by the male respondents during the Antisar watershed development programme.**

N=284

| Sr. No. | Constraints | Percentage |
|---|---|---|
| | **(A) Economical Constraints:** | |
| 1. | Lack of finance | 86.26 |
| 2. | High cost involved in adoption of technology | 84.50 |
| 3. | Lack of marketing facilities | 50.00 |
| | **(B) Technological Constraints:** | |
| 4. | Lack of knowledge about watershed management practices. | 65.49 |
| 5. | Complexity of technology | 59.15 |
| 6. | Lack of technical guidance. | 55.98 |
| | **(C) Input Availability Constraints:** | |
| 7. | Shortage of labour in watershed | 75.00 |
| 8. | Inadequate transport facilities | 65.14 |
| 9. | Inadequate availability of inputs needed | 46.47 |
| | **(D) Situational Constraints:** | |
| 10. | Lack of cooperation of people | 62.32 |
| 11. | Lack of good leadership in the watershed | 55.63 |
| 12. | Political interference | 52.81 |
| 13. | Factionalism of population | 40.49 |

The data of the table 50 revealed that the majority of the male respondents faced the constraints during Antisar watershed development programme. The important constraints faced by the male respondents were lack of finance, high cost involved in adoption of technology, shortage of labour in watershed area, lack of knowledge about watershed management practices, inadequate transport facilities and lack of cooperation of people.

**Constraints faced by the female respondents:**

**Table 51: Itemwise percentage distribution and rank order of constraints faced by the female respondents during the Antisar watershed development programme.**

N=108

| Sr. No. | Constraints | Percentage |
|---|---|---|
| | **(A) Economical Constraints:** | |
| 1. | Lack of finance | 92.59 |
| 2. | High cost involved in adoption of technology | 85.18 |
| 3. | Lack of marketing facilities | 42.59 |
| | **(B) Technological Constraints:** | |
| 4. | Lack of knowledge about watershed management practices. | 84.25 |
| 5. | Lack of technical guidance. | 63.88 |
| 6. | Complexity of technology | 61.14 |
| | **(C) Input Availability Constraints:** | |
| 7. | Shortage of labour in watershed | 88.88 |
| 8. | Inadequate transport facilities | 70.37 |
| 9. | Inadequate availability of inputs needed | 52.45 |
| | **(D) Situational Constraints:** | |
| 10. | Lack of cooperation of people | 78.70 |
| 11. | Lack of good leadership in the watershed | 64.81 |
| 12. | Political interference | 59.61 |
| 13. | Factionalism of population | 35.18 |

The data of table 51 revealed that majority of the female respondents also faced the constraints during Antisar watershed development programme. The important constraints faced by them were lack of finance, shortage of labour in watershed, high cost involved in adoption of technology, lack of knowledge about watershed management practices, lack of cooperation of people and inadequate transport facilities.

The above findings may lead us to conclude that due attention and importance need to be granted to take care of the constraints faced by farmers. A due priority should be decided for each of them so that more crucial constraints may be resolved quickly, to prevent damage of any kind to the programme and also to ensure its smooth function.

The Spearman ranks coefficient of correlation $p^{(rho)}$ was calculated in the study to measure the correlation in between the ranks assigned by the male and female respondents to the constraints faced by them during the developmental stages of the Antisar watershed project. The Spearman ranks coefficient of correlation was calculated as 0.962, which is highly significantly correlated. This means the problems faced by both the male and female respondents are on most grounds similar and identical.

**Conclusion of the study:**
1. The findings of this study revealed that majority of both the male and female respondents had belonged to middle age group having medium to small size of land holdings with primary level of education. The respondents were having medium socio-economic status and moderate level of social participation by male farmers and low level of social participation by female farmers.
2. The study also revealed that the majority of respondents had moderate farm power.
3. The findings revealed that majority of male and female farmers had moderate level of risk preference towards adoption of SWC technologies.
4. The findings with regards to knowledge of male and female farmers about soil and water conservation technologies indicated that they had moderate level of knowledge.
5. It was revealed that majority of respondents had neutral attitude towards SWC programmes.
6. The findings with regards to adoption of SWC technologies indicated that the male and female farmers had medium level of adoption.
7. The findings revealed that majority of the rural male and female farmers had moderate level of participation in planning of SWC programme.
8. People's participation in implementation stage of soil and water conservation programme was found moderate level by the male and female farmers.
9. The result of the study have revealed that majority of male and female farmers had moderate level of participation in maintenance of SWC programme.
10. The study revealed that the male farmers with more socio-economic status, large land holdings, more farm power, big family size, more social participation, risk preference, knowledge, attitude and adoption exhibits more people's participation in SWC programme.
11. The study also revealed that the female farmers with high socio-economic status, more education, big family size, more social participation and more risk preference with good knowledge and favourable attitude towards SWC programme exhibits more participation in SWC programme.

## CHAPTER 4

# PARTICIPATORY APPROACH BASED ON DISCUSSION OF FINDINGS

## DISCUSSION OF FINDINGS

This deals with the discussion of the findings on the study of the selected characteristics of male and female farmers of Antisar watershed of Gujarat.

## 4.1 PROFILE OF THE RESPONDENTS

The findings of this study reveal that majority of respondents both the male and female belong to the middle age group. The physical and psychological development of an individual is related to his or her age. It influences interests and needs of rural farmers. It plays a vital role in acquiring knowledge and know-how about soil and water conservation technologies and thereby it helps in developing favourable attitude towards SWC practices. Therefore, the middle age group might have better health and ability to do construction of soil and water conservation structures on their land for sustainable.

It is usually found that the middle age group take up their parental occupation and as a result, farming is left in the hands of old people. Old farmers being physically slow and weak may not be able to carry out different hard agricultural operations in the fields. Old farmers should preferably play a supporting role by imparting counselling based on their experiences. Hence, the middle age and young age rural people, male as well as female farmers should be given priority in such soil and water conservation programmes on watershed management. Young rural farmers should be contacted frequently to motivate them to participate in planning and execution of soil and water conservation works on their own land and on the land owned by their community. The young generation holds modern approach and enthusiasm to adopt new technologies, whereas the old generation farmers adhere to traditional practices.

The study reveals that the respondents in Antisar watershed area possess middle socio-economic status. It might be due to fact that majority of farmers have moderate infrastructure facilities to carry on agricultural operations on their field. The socio-economic status of rural farmers has direct bearing on the development of agriculture. It reflects upon the infrastructural facilities that the farmers have to carry out different agricultural operations. Rural farmers should always seek to develop their infrastructural facilities like farm implements, equipment, farm machinery, farm materials etc.

Majority of the farmers in Antisar watershed area possess moderate to high degree of farm power. It means that they very well know that the farm power is an essential input to carry out various operations. The farm power is a major input required for cultivation operations in agriculture. Agricultural machines like tractor, trailer, water pumpset etc. are essential equipments. Agricultural implements such as ploughs, cultivator, thresher, seed drill, chaff cutter etc. are also much useful in agricultural production operations. The farmers in Antisar watershed area make use of different kinds of farm machinery and farm implements to carry out cultivation operations. These implements and machinery are also useful in the construction of the SWC technologies on their fields. This implies that the farmers should keep up high farm power, which may be useful even in the soil and water conservation works to ensure sustainable agricultural production.

In order to keep up high farm power, one needs good finance to invest. The farmers may not have adequate finance for the purpose. Hence, it is also essential that loan facilities are made available to farmers who need financial support to purchase farm machines and farm implements, as the case may be.

It is usually seen that agricultural land is divided into small pieces to distribute among the children who inherited it from their parents. The farmers in the Antisar watershed area are found to be cultivating small or medium sized land-pieces owned by them on individual ground. They are not inclined to do farming on cooperative basis farming group of their fellow-farmers.

The soil and water conservation technologies are adopted in most cases on the basis of contour lines of the land. The soil and water conservation can be planned in better way on watershed basis only. Large sized land holdings are conducive for adoption of the SWC practices. Hence, the farmers who have small farm holdings need to carry out agricultural cultivation on collective grounds on the basis of watershed area. It would, therefore, be better if children inheriting small land pieces unite with others of the kind and cultivate their land on collective basis rather than to divide the land into small pieces.

It is again noticed that illiteracy prevails among the farmers of the Antisar watershed area. The level of education among them is very low. The probable reason for low education among them is poverty. Poor economic conditions and non-availability of schools and colleges in rural areas go hand in hand. The farmers might have preferred to send their children to fields to raise livelihood and support the family. Right from the childhood, children are thus deprived of education at schools. In such cases, colleges and higher education remain mere myth for them. There are schools upto primary levels in small villages. They do not have adequate facilities. Farmers can not afford to send their children to schools and colleges in cities. Hence, it is highly required that the condition of village schools should be improved and farmers should be motivated to send their children to schools for education.

The farmers in Antisar watershed area possess medium to small sized land holdings. Therefore, the income from the agricultural production is also small. The income of farmers might be low also due to lack of irrigation facilities for crop cultivation in the summer season. Most farmers in the area have rainfed farming only. The annual average rainfall in the Antisar watershed area is below 500 mm. The resulting cropping intensity in the area is also low. It is, therefore, highly desirable that the farmers should adopt the soil and water conservation structures for water recharging of land. It may increase the availability of water in wells in summer season. Consequently, agricultural production may also be increased.

Money plays a vital role in the planning of multipurpose activities. Particularly, in adoption of soil and water conservation technologies, the initial cost of adoption is very high. Money also allows timely procurement of inputs or materials required for adoption of soil and water conservation technologies. The farmers should have easy access to local financial institutions from where they avail required amount on loans for adoption of new technologies.

The low level of education among the farmer in Antisar watershed area results into moderate social participation from male respondents and low social participation from female respondents. They are unable to understand the importance of village organizations such as village Panchayat, cooperative societies, milk cooperative societies, village bank etc. Men toil through out the day on their lands. Women remain ever busy with household work and caring for the family. They also hesitate to talk with people due to restrictions imposed by the customs prevailing in Indian rural societies. Social participation among them is either very low or absent.

Social participation allows on extent to which an individual farmer can actively involve in the affairs of rural development institutions. If farmers and farm women have enough contacts with rural social organizations, they may be exposed to and motivated to cultivate interest in soil and water conservation programmes. They should also be motivated for more and more social participation so that they may acquire more knowledge and awareness about different rural development programmes in the area. Social participation helps farmers and farm women to know about village organizations and to be aware of their role in rural development.

## 4.2 RISK PREFERENCE OF FARMERS TOWARDS SWC TECHNOLOGIES

The findings of the study revealed that majority of farmers in Antisar watershed area have moderate to high risk preference regarding adoption of new soil and water conservation technologies for land recharging and sustainable agricultural production. This finding goes on the line of the findings presented by Trivedi (1984), Bhatt (1990) and Gamit (1993).

Trivedi (1984) conducted a research study on transfer of agricultural technologies among tribal farmers of Panchmahals district of Gujarat State. He reported that majority of the tribal respondents had medium (53.89 per cent) to high (25.00 per cent) risk preference. About 21.00 per cent had low risk preference.

Bhatt (1990) carried out a research study on transfer of hybrid maize technologies among the tribal farmers of Girwa block in Udaipur district of the Rajasthan State. He also reported that majority of the tribal respondents (71.66 per cent) were found to have medium risk preference followed by those (17.34 per cent) who had low and those (11.00 per cent) who had high risk preferences.

Gamit (1993) conducted a research study on extent of adoption of recommended summer groundnut technology by the tribal farmers of the Panchmahals district of the Gujarat State. The study revealed that majority (71.67 per cent) of tribal respondents had medium risk bearing ability.

Majority of male and female farmers observe moderate to high level of risk preference. The possible reason is that they are oriented to face risk and uncertainty towards survival of soil and water conservation structures on their fields due to high intensity rainfall, long duration rainfall, drought and high cost involved in adoption of soil and water conservation technologies. The agricultural cultivation is the basic occupation of these farmers. Therefore, they might take risk of the adoption of new SWC technologies in the interest of increase in agricultural production. The farmers might have faith in the project implementing agency and extension personnel who would bring to them new SWC technologies. They might even be motivated to adopt the new SWC technologies in degraded fields for crop cultivation and increased production, even if they are costly (expensive) agricultural occupation as such usually involve many risk factors. Hence, the farmers develop a tendency of taking risks.

Agriculture is characterized by many uncontrollable variables such as rainfall, diseases and price fluctuations etc. Therefore, there is a risk in adoption of new soil and water conservation measures that are costly. Hence, male and female farmers in villages must hold courage to take risk in adoption of new soil and water conservation measures. The unproductive and waste ravine lands can be converted into cultivable and productive lands if they adopt soil and water conservation measures. The farmers should not hesitate to adopt new although costly, soil and water conservation measures in ravine lands in the interest of increase in agricultural production. They should be motivated to replace their old traditional methods with new improved soil and water conservation methods. And farmers on their part should be enthusiastic to adopt SWC practices even if they yield benefits in the long term rather than yielding immediate returns.

## 4.3 KNOWLEDGE LEVELS OF RESPONDENTS REGARDING SWC TECHNOLOGIES

The present study shows that the majority of the respondents have moderate level of knowledge regarding soil and water conservation technologies.

Similar findings were also reported by the researchers like Prabhu and Kadam (1990), Patel (1991) and Nandrana (1994).

Prabhu and Kadam (1990) state that majority of the adopters and non-adopters had medium level of knowledge on soil conservation practices. About one fifth of both the categories of farmers had low level of knowledge. Hardly thirty per cent (30%) of non-adopters were found to be having high level of knowledge.

Patel (1991) conducted a study of farmers' knowledge about soil and water conservation measures. He found that a large majority of the respondents (73.33%) belonged to medium level of knowledge category. They were followed by some 16.67 per cent and 10.00 per cent of respondents who belonged to groups of high and low level of knowledge respectively.

Nandrana (1994) reported farmers' knowledge about water conservation practices. He found that majority of the respondents (60%) had medium level of knowledge. Whereas some 24.00 and 16.00 per cent of them had respectively low and high level of knowledge about improved water conservation practices.

The possible reasons for having moderate level of knowledge among farmers might be lack of awareness about soil and water conservation technologies and lack of training facilities in that regards in villages. The construction of SWC structures require technical knowledge.

The implications of the above findings are that the knowledge level of farmers in rural areas regarding soil and water conservation technologies is an important aspect that plays vital role in adoption of soil and water conservation programme. In order to increase the knowledge level of farmers in soil and water conservation programmes, the rural farmers must be aware of the recent knowledge regarding soil and water conservation technologies. It is also understood that if farmers have more knowledge about soil and water conservation technologies, they might contribute considerably to an increased participation in soil and water conservation programme. The male and female farmers in villages must have enough contacts with and visits to different soil and water conservation institutions by which they may acquire more learning about conservation measures. The soil and water conservation institutes as well should organize soil and water conservation training programmes for rural farmers so that they may improve their skill regarding soil and water conservation technologies. The soil and water conservation training programmes must be suitable to specific conservation problems and situations of the farmers.

## 4.4 ATTITUDE OF FARMERS TOWARDS SWC PROGRAMME

It is revealed from the present study that majority of the male and female respondents had neutral attitude towards participation in the SWC programme.

The attitude of farmers towards soil and water conservation programmes also exerts influence on adoption of natural resource conservation measures.

The farmers who have favourable attitude towards soil and water conservation programme can easily adopt soil and water conservation technologies. The other researchers were also reported findings on attitude towards soil and water conservation.

Reddy's study (1987) reveals that majority of the respondents exhibit more favourable attitude towards all the three components viz., (i) soil and water conservation (ii) improved dry farming technology and (iii) non-arable land development of WDP. Moreover, the study reveals that there is a significant difference between big and small farmers in their overall attitude towards watershed management practices. The big farmers form a more favourable attitude towards all the three components of watershed management than small farmers do.

Patel's study (1991) finds that majority of the respondent (75.71%) held favourable attitude to the SWC programme, whereas some 12.39 % of them held highly favourable attitude and some 11.90% of them held less favourable attitude towards the watershed development programme.

The probable reason of neutral attitude of farmers towards soil and water conservation programme on watershed basis might be lack of knowledge and awareness among them about soil and water conservation measures. Lack of education keeps them busy in the different agricultural operations in which knowledge is not the requirement. They participate very little in the soil and water conservation programme and planning meetings. They put forth very little of their suggestions regarding points of their own interest in the planning of SWC programme and that too with much hesitation. Farmers in villages usually believe that such type of rural development programmes are government programmes and the project implementing authority is totally responsible for the management of development activities. In this part, they have nothing to do. But it is a mere false notion on their part.

It is, therefore, suggested that more effective extension strategy should be tailored to generate awareness among the rural farmers so that they cultivate apt understanding of the SWC programme on watershed basis. Such programmes should be managed by farmers, for farmers and of farmers. Activities addressing to farmers' need should be incorporated in the watershed development programme. It will encourage in them favourable attitude to the programme. The integrated watershed development programme has to meet the basic needs like food, fodder and fuel of local farmers both male and female. It has to be noted that to enhance the favourable attitude of farmers towards watershed development programme, there should prevail common understanding between farmers and the project implementing agency through healthy discussion and interactions in relation to different developmental activities to be undertaken during watershed management.

Further, rural farmers should be motivated to participate favourably in planning, implementation and maintenance of soil and water conservation programme through contributing labour, money and experience. It may be in the form of public recognition through public functions to honour them, announcement of prizes and ranks and publicizing them through the media and also putting them in responsible positions to contribute from their experience to the programme.

## **4.5** ADOPTION OF SWC TECHNOLOGIES

It is revealed from the study that majority of the respondents had medium level adoption of soil and water conservation technologies, very few per cent had low and high level adoption. Other researchers like Padmiah (1992) and Bhutiya (1993) give out similar findings.

Padmiah et al. (1992) observes that majority of farmers in the watershed area (52.00%) fell into medium adoption level group. They were followed by high adoption level group (34.00%) and low adoption level group (14.00%). In case of farmers outside the watershed area, the majority of respondents (66.00%) belonged to a medium adoption level group. They were followed by those under a low adoption level group with 34.00 per cent.

Bhutiya (1993) observes that majority of adopter farmers (73.00%) were found to be in a medium adoption category. They were followed by a high level adoption category (30.00%). There was none in a category of low level adoption with respect to the watershed management programme. In case of non-adopter farmers, majority of the respondents (70.77%) were found to be in a medium level adoption category and some 28.33 per cent of them were in a low level adoption category, while hardly 1.67 per cent of the non-adopter farmers showed high level of adoption with respect to the watershed management programme.

The reasons for this trend may be lack of soil and water conservation technologies, lack of its knowledge, high cost involved in adoption of soil and water conservation technologies and non-suitability of the SWC technologies to the field conditions of rural areas. Adoption of soil and water conservation technologies also depends on economic condition and resource availability with the farmers. The situation and size of a field is also a vital consideration for adoption of soil and water conservation technologies, because small land holdings are unsuitable for adoption of the SWC structure.

The implications of the findings are that intensive educational and motivational efforts have to be undertaken by the implementing agency in order to enhance the adoption level of soil and water conservation practices on watershed basis. Input resources such as construction materials, implements and labour required for construction of soil and water conservation structures should also be made available to farmers. It is also important that both male and female farmers should realize the importance of soil and water conservation measures on watershed basis in the interest of increasing sustainable agricultural production. The soil and water conservation technologies should be developed according to the suitability of the area. Therefore, enhancement of educational facilities in rural areas and suitable low cost or no cost soil and water conservation technologies for rural farmers are most desirous factors that would work for easy transfer of soil and water conservation innovations in rural areas.

## **4.6 PEOPLE'S PARTICIPATION IN SWC PROGRAMME**

It is revealed that majority of male and female respondents exhibit moderate level of participation in planning, implementation and maintenance stages of soil and water conservation programme for sustainable agricultural production. Similar findings regarding people's participation in rural development programme are also reported in studies by researchers like Sen (1986), Singh (1988), Suresh (1990) and Kulkarni (1991).

Sen (1986) conducted a study on people's participation in community forestry– a case study in Maharashtra, in Aurangabad circle of Northern Maharashtra. There has been quite a number of plantation taken up during the last decade. The social forestry department initiated several plantations in this region. Some plantations have also been taken up under the United States Aid assisted project.

The study concludes that the strategy for planning and implementation of rural development programme needed review. It should be tailored to render it more effective in achieving the objectives of the programme, once it is accepted as community welfare programme. It is suggested that the approach should cover the dual perspective of providing short-term as well as long-term benefits to the rural community. In an effort to reach such goals, community education is of vital significance, which will motivate them to increasingly participate in the programme.

Singh's study conducted in 1988 concludes that the women are the backbone of the hill agriculture undertaken in the area of participation of rural farm women in agriculture in the hills of Uttar Pradesh. Men associated with it only for the tasks like ploughing and marketing of agricultural produces. Women play a positive role in decision making. But men who are playing a dominate role in the process of decision making. This pattern of work and role distribution (division of labour) between males and females exert heavy impact directly and indirectly.

Suresh in his study (1990) reveals that the rates of participation of beneficiaries and institutional arrangements for participation are found to be very low in majority of organizations in Kerala. The beneficiaries are not taken into confidence at several stages of planning and implementation of programmes that are basically meant for them. The beneficiaries are also found to be resentful in actively involved in decision making bodies and planning processes. The institutional arrangements for participation and the participation scores are as such directly correlated. Hence, more vigorous and more sustainable efforts are needed to incorporate such arrangements in all the development organizations and their programmes.

Kulkarni (1991) conducted a study on participation of rural farm women in decision making in different agricultural operations. It reveals that the role played by rural women in decision making is apparent, but it is accepted indirectly in the form of suggestion. This is due to dominance of men in the affairs of families by tradition, which is still prevalent.

The reason for moderate level of farmers' participation in soil and water conservation programme is lack of awareness among them about soil and water conservation rural development programmes. Lack of education among farmers and lack of knowledge in them render them ignorant about their rights and privileges, duties and responsibilities in the soil and water conservation programme on watershed basis.

The farmers may participate very little in the soil and water conservation programme, planning meetings and they suggest very little on points of their own interest in the planning of such SWC programme. The rural farmers perhaps think that such type of rural development programmes are government programmes and the project implementing authority has to carry out responsibility of implementation of different development activities in the watershed area.

The moderate level of participation might probably be due to initial high cost involved in adoption of the soil and water conservation technologies and the non-suitability of the SWC technologies to the field conditions of the rural farmers. The topographic situation and the size of a field are valid factors responsible for adoption of soil and water conservation technologies, because small land holdings are not conducive to adoption of the SWC structures.

It is also found that local rural organizations like panchayats, cooperatives, mahila mandals, and youth clubs take little or no interest in the SWC programmes. Farmers also lack good leadership that would motivate them to participate in the watershed development programmes. Thus, lack of interest, involvement, motivation and guidance result significantly in farmers' absenteeism in participation of SWC programmes and its implementation.

The implications of the findings are that the participation should be conceived as a major component of the development programme from its very inception. There is a need to ensure that all caste groups are given adequate representation in soil and water conservation development programmes. The first and foremost objective of the programme should be to satisfy farmers' basic needs viz., fuel, fodder and food. Once this is taken care, they would come forward to involve them actively in the programme.

All possible efforts should be made to educate people on various aspects of the soil and water conservation programme and their significance to their interest, so that they would get a clear idea about the nature of various aspects of the programme. This would enable them to organize themselves into small functional groups.

People's involvement in the activity is influenced by the literacy rate among them. Therefore, provision of education, formal and informal, to all people is as essential as water and food. It is the first requisite to be attended on. This would enhance the capacity of people to plan schemes and to initiate and follow-up them.

The existing rural organizations like panchayats, cooperatives, mahila mandals, and youth clubs should be activated and welfare programmes meant for the community should be routed through these organizations.

The farmers should be motivated to develop attitude that soil and water conservation development programmes are their own programmes and such programmes are meant for the farmers, to be managed by the farmers and to be owned by them. They should be educated that the project implementing authority is not totally responsible for such programmes. They have to share responsibility with the authority to generate and safeguard their interests.

Farmers who are involved in the soil and water conservation development programme should be made aware about their rights, privileges, duties and responsibilities, so that they can participate very well meaningfully. Leaders play an important role as facilitators in a process of change. There is a need to identify leaders who are informal, yet influential in the community and who have vital influence over local farmers. Such leaders should be selected and trained in all schemes of the development programme.

## 4.7 RELATIONSHIP BETWEEN THE OVERALL PARTICIPATION AND SELECTED VARIABLES

**Relationship between the overall males' participation in soil and water conservation programme and selected independent variables:**

The findings of the present study revealed that by increase in the socio-economic status of farmers, land holding, farm power, family size, social participation, risk preference, knowledge regarding SWC practices, favourable attitude towards SWC programme and adoption of soil and water conservation technologies, increases the overall participation of male farmers in soil and water conservation programme.

It might be due to the fact that if rural male farmers enjoy high level of socio-economic status, they may afford to have more resources to their disposal. Financially sound position may encourage them for participation in planning, implementation and maintenance of SWC structures on their land. The improved socio economic status of farmers enables them to have improved infrastructure facilities on their lands to carry out construction of conservation structures. The farmers having higher socio economic status are capable of participating more and more in the SWC programmes by contributing resources. They are also able to contribute with more and more available physical facilities such as implements, equipment, material etc. when the implementation and maintenance of soil and water conservation programmes are undertaken.

As stated earlier, large size of land holding is the primary requirement for adoption of different SWC structures. The reason is the soil and water conservation technologies are adopted on the basis of contour lines in the watershed area. The soil and water conservation can be planned in better way on the watershed basis only. For such reason, big farmers may be able to participate more in the soil and water conservation programme.

Farm powers such as animal power, mechanical power, irrigation facilities and farm implements etc. help farmers in participation. They also carry out the construction work during adoption of different soil and water conservation structures in the watershed.

If the number of persons in a family of a rural male farmer is more he might get a chance to involve himself more in soil and water conservation works and in adoption and maintenance of different Soil and water conservation structures. Therefore, farmers should prefer joint farming system with other farmers in their watershed area and choose to adopt the soil and water conservation technologies collectively on watershed basis.

Social participation allows one frequent contacts with rural village institutions. More social participation helps male farmers in more participation in planning of soil and water conservation programme. Rural male farmers who have more contacts with rural village institution and extension agencies keep abreast of the latest innovations regarding soil and water conservation. They also receive help and guidance as and when they need in adoption of different soil and water conservation structures.

Rural male farmers with high-risk preferences are oriented towards maximization of income from agriculture. They take risk in adoption of different new improved soil and water conservation structures on their land.

Rural male farmers who have better knowledge of soil and water conservation technologies are likely to utilize the knowledge for participation in planning, implementation and maintenance of soil and water conservation structures on their land. In turn, their work generates more income. The more knowledgeable male farmers are regarding SWC practices, the easier would be for them to participate in the SWC programme.

The male farmers with more favourable attitude towards soil and water conservation programme are likely to allow the project implementing authority to implement the soil and water conservation programme on their land as well as on the land owned by their community. They might have more meaningful contribution and participation in planning, implementation and maintenance of soil and water conservation programme in their village.

If rural male farmers show behaviour of high adoption regarding soil and water conservation technologies, they are likely to learn more and more to maintain the already-adopted SWC structures on their farm by more participation in planning, implementation and maintenance of soil and water conservation programme.

The findings in the present study also reveal that the age, education and income are found to be non-significantly correlated with overall participation of male farmers in soil and water conservation programme.

It is also a fact that old age male farmers in villages are weak in physical ability. They are unable to render active participation in soil and water conservation programmes. Although, these old farmers possess knowledge and experience of traditional SWC practices that they have adopted for long time, they are too rigid to change and adopt to new SWC technologies. Younger farmers on the other hand, participate more in the soil and water conservation. They impart higher and active contribution through more labour work than old farmers can do. The young age farmers have good physical strength to carry out hard toiling and tasks on a land during implementation and construction of soil and water conservation structures on their farm. Whereas, old farmers are very weak in physical strength and due to it they can not contribute labour work during construction of SWC structures.

Education level among majority of rural male farmers is found to be upto the primary level. Educated farmers are interested more in taking up jobs or businesses rather than to choose agriculture as their main occupation. Therefore, educated farmers should be motivated to adopt agriculture as their main occupation for livelihood.

Rich farmers have higher annual income. It is possible that they are not interested to take up agricultural operations and contribute their own labour. They take it as sporting their prestige in the society and the village. Looking to their high socio-economic status, they hire labourers from nearby villages to carry out their agricultural operations on their fields.

## Relationship between the overall females' participation in soil and water conservation programme and selected independent variables:

It is as well revealed from the study that increase in the socio-economic status, education, family size, social participation, risk preference, knowledge regarding SWC practices and favourable attitude towards SWC programme increases the overall participation of female farmers in soil and water conservation programme.

The fact that rural female farmers enjoy high socio-economic status will have then more resources at their disposal to participate in planning, implementation and maintenance of SWC programme.

If the female farmers in villages possess high level of education they can have more effective participation in planning, implementation and maintenance of SWC programme. In villages, educated women possess more knowledge about agriculture and are more capable of taking decisions about agricultural operations. Therefore, educated women in rural area may be able to contribute to more meaningful participation in soil and water conservation programme planning, implementation as well as in its maintenance.

If women in villages have more members in their families, they may get better chance to involve themselves in participation in soil and water conservation programme in planning, implementation and in maintenance of different soil and water conservation structures. They might also extend more of helping hands in agricultural development works. This implies that the farmers should work on collective ground with cooperation to each other in agricultural operations.

The rural female farmers who have more personal contacts with rural village institution and extension agencies can explore ready contacts with latest innovations in soil and water conservation. They can come forward to participate more actively. They also receive help and guidance from competent persons or authority as and when they need in adoption of different soil and water conservation structures.

The rural female farmers were oriented towards higher risk preference with a view to maximizing their income from agriculture by adopting new soil and water conservation structures on their land.

It is again understood that if female farmers in villages have better knowledge level in respect to soil and water conservation technologies, they can utilize that knowledge for participation in planning, implementation and maintenance of soil and water conservation structures on their land and generate more income.

The female farmers with more favourable attitude towards soil and water conservation programme are likely to allow and cooperate project implementing authority in effective implementation of soil and water conservation programme on their land. They might also have more contribution through participation in planning, implementation and maintenance of soil and water conservation programme in their villages.

It is also revealed that with increase in the income of the female farmers, their overall participation decreased. It is worth noting that in case of rural female farmers the income is found negatively and significantly correlated with the female's overall participation in the soil and water conservation programme. It is because of it that the rich women avoid contributing through their own labour and any kind of participation in planning, implementation and maintenance in soil and water conservation programme. They treat it to affect adversely their prestige in the society and the village. Rich families in the rural areas even object to any involvement of female members in agricultural operations or any kind of work in their fields. They prefer to hire agricultural labourers to manage agricultural operations on their fields. It is also because of the social prestige, rich male farmers do not allow their women to take part in village level meetings. Social customs and prestige prevent them. This implies that rich female farmers in the rural areas should be motivated to contribute with their own labour and money in planning, implementation and maintenance of soil and water conservation programme.

The findings of the present study also revealed that in case of female farmers as their age increased their overall participation in the programme decreased. Whereas, any increase in land holding, farm power and adoption of SWC practices improves their overall participation of female farmers.

It is revealed that the age is negatively and non-significantly correlated with overall participation of female farmers in the soil and water conservation programme. It means by increasing the age of female farmers the participation decreases. There may be another reason also that old rural women are weak in physical ability and unable to perform and participate effectively in the soil and water conservation programmes. They even object to or prevent other young female women in their families to participate in planning of such programmes. Rural women can not enter into open discussion with the staff of the PIA. Traditional customs prevailing in rural areas prevent any kind of public participation on their part.

The large size of land holdings are conducive for adoption of different soil and water conservation structures. But it does not happen because male farmers take all the decisions regarding different cultivation operations on the land and female farmers have just to follow the decision taken by male farmers in the family. The male dominate the decision power and the female are reduced to just passive followers in an Indian social set up. This very factor affects the female initiative and participation in the matter.

The farm powers viz. animal power, mechanical power, irrigation facilities, and farm implements etc. may help women in participation and adoption of different soil and water conservation structures. However, it would be difficult and not practical for them to operate directly and handle animals and farm machinery during agricultural operations.

The rural female farmers who are more willing to adopt soil and water conservation technologies are likely to learn more to maintain the structures once they are adopted on their fields. They may even participate more willingly in planning, implementation and maintenance of soil and water conservation programme. It may also be true once the reclamation of land is completed, the adoption of SWC practices may not be required further with the same soil and water conservation practices. Thus, the programme may not have the repeat value.

## 4.8 RELATIONSHIP BETWEEN THE PARTICIPATION IN PLANNING AND VARIABLES

**Relationship between the males' participation in planning of soil and water conservation programme and selected independent variables:**

An analysis of the findings reveal that as the socio-economic status, land holding, farm power, social participation, risk preference, knowledge and attitude towards SWC programme increases, the participation of male farmers in planning of soil and water conservation programme too increases on considerable ground.

The socio-economic status of farmers reflects on the resources in their possession. The farmers who have a higher socio economic status and possess more resources mobility in the local area are capable to cultivate more contacts with and extend higher participation to the project implementing agency. The socio-economic status is thus, directly or indirectly correlated with the participation of farmers in the planning. Male farmers with the high socio-economic status can participate in planning meetings with greater confidence and power and maintain their dominance in the village. They take greater interest in decision taking process as need arises in order to derive more benefits and advantages from the SWC programme.

Big size of land holding is also a vital factor to enable farmers to participate more significantly, because the soil and water conservation has the prerequisite to maintain a big size of land holding. It helps to check the soil erosion. Further, the soil and water conservation technologies are adopted on watershed contour lines basis and large size land holdings are conducive and more suitable for adoption of different SWC structures. Big farmers may have meaningful participation in soil and water conservation planning meetings if they agree to maintain big land holdings. They also show active interest in taking decisions and planning meetings to as much extent as they need to derive benefits from SWC programme. Therefore, big size of land holding enables rich farmers to participate more effectively in planning of soil and water conservation programme.

Farm power is also significantly correlated with participation in planning by male farmers. Farm power in the form of animal power, mechanical power, irrigation facilities, and farm implements help male farmers in construction of soil and water conservation structures on their land. Therefore, if farmers have more farm power, They can participate easily in planning and adoption of soil and water conservation structures on their land. Possession of more farm power and implements can help the rural male farmers to participate in planning meetings of soil and water conservation programme. They also enable them to take decisions for adoption of conservation structures on their farm land. Farmers who are interested in agricultural development usually keep and maintain more farm power to carry out different operations on their fields. With more farm power farmers may show more interest in planning of SWC programme so that they can learn more to use their farm power in the programme. Farmers having more farm power, thus, may exhibit more participation in planning. They can adopt SWC structures on their farm more effectively with the help of farm implements in their possession. They also participate to take decisions to adopt improved SWC structures on their fields.

Social participation paves the way for farmers' involvement in the affairs of rural institutions. Farmers develop more relationship and contacts with rural social organization. They are expected to involve actively with their contacts in planning of soil and water conservation programme. The possible reason could be that rural male farmers, who have more contacts with officials of rural village institutions and extension agencies can contribute with more meaningful participation in planning of SWC programme.

Male farmers showing higher risk preference are usually oriented to maximization of income from agriculture. They are eager to adopt on their lands different new soil and water conservation structures that promise them good return of their investment. Therefore, the farmers with more risk taking ability assure higher contribution and more active participation in planning for the adoption of SWC structures on their land as well as on a land owned by the community.

Knowledge level of rural male farmers counts as vital factor. Farmers' interest and knowledge of soil and water conservation technologies is highly positively and significantly correlated with males' participation in planning of soil and water conservation programme. It is indeed understood rural male farmers with better knowledge level regarding soil and water conservation technologies are likely to utilize their knowledge in planning of soil and water conservation programme on their land. It would further help them to generate more income. Such farmers can exchange their ideas through interactions and discussions in planning meetings. They can as well motivate other fellow farmers to adopt the SWC programme.

Male farmers who hold more favourable attitude towards soil and water conservation programme are likely to allow project-implementing authority to affect planning and implementation of soil and water conservation programme on their land. They will also have more meaningful contribution and participation in planning of soil and water conservation programme in their village.

It was also revealed from the findings that increase in age, family size, income and adoption increases in participation of male farmers in the soil and water conservation programme non-significantly. Whereas, any increase in the level of education reduces the participation in soil and water conservation programme non-significantly on the part of male farmers.

It is also a fact that rural male farmers in their old age suffer from poor health conditions. They are, therefore, unable to perform actively and participate effectively in planning of soil and water conservation programme. Old age farmers are usually rigid to any change. They prefer to adhere to old traditional practices. They usually resent to attend meetings of soil and water conservation planning and to adopt new technologies. They remain too idle or lethargic to attend to any important work of agriculture cultivation that involves hard labour. They take rest in their homes and involve very little even in the domestic work. When the need arises they may do work with very little will. Despite all these conditions, it is an undeniable fact that old farmers possess good traditional experience. Yet, low awareness among them about new soil and water conservation practices would render them little effective to help the programme.

Education among rural male farmers was found negatively and non-significantly correlated with the their participation in planning of the SWC programme. It might be due to the fact that the majority of male farmers reach upto primary education level only. It is also true that the educated young male farmers are more interested in jobs and businesses rather than in agriculture. They attach remotest preference to cultivation as occupation. Therefore, educated rural population should be motivated and encouraged to adopt agriculture as their occupation. Educated young generation of rural farmers do not like to participate in planning and to take decisions for agriculture development programmes. They also lack practical experience in agriculture and do not have adequate ideas and skills to share with their fellow farmers in the SWC programme.

When the male family members in a rural family are more, they could be involve them in soil and water conservation works and in adoption of different soil and water conservation structures. However, the finding was revealed positive but non-significant.

Rich farmers with higher income might have already adopted the soil and water conservation structures on their farm. It is because of it that the rich farmers do not desire to take actual part in planning of soil and water conservation structures. It is also because their farm lands are developed they do not require again adoption of soil and water conservation structures. Income and males' participation in planning are factors known to be non-significantly correlated. Further, the finance required to meet the cost of adoption and construction of soil and water conservation structures in a farmer's field is too high for him to afford. Those farmers whose income is higher can participate more in planning according to their needs, in adoption of SWC structures on their field. These farmers can afford high cost involved in adoption of SWC structures. Thus, rich farmers exhibit greater interest in planning meetings.

Rural male farmers were observed to have adoption behaviour regarding soil and water conservation technologies. It was found positively and non-significantly correlated with male's participation in planning of soil and water conservation programme. It is also a fact that the rural male farmers have more adoption of soil and water conservation technologies that are already set up on their land. They are also likely to participate little in planning stage of soil and water conservation programme, because the farmers do not need to adopt SWC practices for reclamation.

## Relationship between the females' participation in planning of soil and water conservation programme and selected independent variables:

In relation to female farmers, it was noticed that with increase in their socio-economic status, social participation, knowledge and attitude towards the SWC programme, their participation in planning of the soil and water conservation programme increased considerably. Whereas, the female farmers' income was more tend to resent to participation in planning of soil and water conservation programme.

This indicates that female farmers in villages who enjoy high level of socio-economic status have more participation in planning of the SWC programme. Women in rural area particularly those who are socially and economically sound are likely to take part in planning of SWC programme. When female farmers own more resources viz. implements, machines, materials etc. they can participate more in planning and take decisions, they would ensure that the resources are used properly in adoption of SWC technologies.

The rural female farmers who are capable of exploring and maintaining more and more contacts with rural village institution and extension agencies, they can be in constant contact with latest innovations regarding soil and water conservation. They also receive good help and guidance from officers and experts, as and when needed, in matter related to adoption of different soil and water conservation structures.

The level of knowledge among rural female farmers regarding soil and water conservation technologies was observed highly positively and significantly correlated with their participation in the planning of soil and water conservation programme. It was also found that if they have better knowledge level regarding soil and water conservation technologies, they are likely to utilize that knowledge for participation in planning of soil and water conservation structures on their land and consequently, generate more income.

If female farmers hold more favourable attitude towards soil and water conservation programme, they are likely to allow and cooperate the project implementing authority in implementation of the soil and water conservation programme on their land. They can also have better contribution in the participation and planning of the soil and water conservation programme in their village.

Income of rural female farmers was found to be negatively and significantly correlated with their participation in the planning of the soil and water conservation programme. Because rich women with higher income do not like to attend and participate a meeting held for the soil and water conservation programme. They belong to rich families and do not like to work in a field. They care more to maintain their status in society. Again, rich male farmers do not allow their women to take part in village level meetings. Further, rich female farmers' land is already levelled and hence, it does not require any adoption of conservation structures.

It was also revealed that as the age of female farmers increased, their participation decreased non-significantly. Whereas, any increase in their land holding, education, farm power, family size, risk preference and adoption mark an increase in participation of female farmers in the planning of the soil and water conservation programme and that is non-significant.

It was further revealed that age plays a negative and non-significant role correlating female farmers' participation in planning of the soil and water conservation programme. It is again a fact that old rural women having weak physical abilities and are unable to perform participation in planning effectively for the soil and water conservation programmes. They even prevent other young women in their family to take part in the planning of such programmes. The old women in villages remain busy all the time with household works. They hardly find time to participate in the planning meetings of the SWC programmes. Old women are also attached to their family and remain busy to caring of the members. The rural women hesitate to take part in planning meeting, to come forward and take decisions. They are too submissive to social customs to act aggressively. They even object to the young women who wish to take part in planning meetings of the SWC programme. The rigidity in a rural society does not allow it.

If female farmers own large sizes of land holding and are financially sound, they exhibit less participation in planning of different soil and water conservation structures on their land. With big land holding they always remain busy in different operations on their land and hardly have find time to take part in planning meetings of the SWC programme.

Education among rural female farmers was found positively and non-significantly correlated with their participation in planning of the SWC programme.

It is due to education that, female farmers hesitate to participate in such programme planning meetings. Educated women do not usually like to adopt agriculture as their occupation. They have a wish to be employed in government or private jobs. They do not have practical skill and knowledge about agricultural operations, because for most time they remain busy in household works and in study. Hence, due to lack of agricultural knowledge they are unable to participate effectively in planning meetings.

The farm powers viz. animal power, mechanical power, irrigation facilities, farm implements etc. ensure for female farmers good participation and meaningful adoption of different soil and water conservation structures on their land. However, it would be difficult for them to handle drought animals and operate farm machinery. Rich women can keep more farm powers, yet they do not like to participate in planning meetings. Traditional customs that prevailing in their rural community stop them to do so.

Large number of members in a family is again a favourable factor to allow women in villages to involve themselves in participation of planning meetings for soil and water conservation. But it turns out to be non-significant. In big families, women are usually busy with nurturing and caring for the members. It is customary in our society that the females carry out this responsibility. It takes most of their time and hardly time left to participate in planning meetings.

Risk preference of rural female farmers was observed as a factor positively and non-significantly correlated with the female participation in planning of the soil and water conservation programme. It is because of it that rural female farmers with higher risk preference are oriented maximization of income raised from agriculture. They can do it by adopting different soil and water conservation structures on their land. But the fact is that all the decisions are taken by male dominating rural society, male farmers take decisions in agricultural development activities on their farm.

It is remarkable to note that if rural female farmers have higher adoption behaviour regarding soil and water conservation technologies, they are likely to learn more to maintain conservation structures by participation in planning of the soil and water conservation programme. But when they have adoption of SWC structures already on their field, their participation in planning meetings is naturally reduced.

## 4.9 RELATIONSHIP BETWEEN THE PARTICIPATION IN IMPLEMENTATION AND VARIABLES

**Relationship between the males' participation in implementation of soil and water conservation programme and selected independent variables:**

The study has revealed that with the increase in the socio-economic status, farm power, risk preference, knowledge and attitude towards SWC programme, the participation of male farmers in implementation of the soil and water conservation programme was also increased significantly.

This indicates that rural male farmers with high level of socio-economic status can have greater participation at the implementation stage with contribution of money or materials. This supports the soil and water conservation programme on watershed basis. A farmer with high socio-economic status means to have more resources, implements, machinery and materials. As a result, they can contribute with implements, machines and materials during the implementation and construction of SWC structures on their land and on a land owned by the community.

Farm powers in the form of animal power, mechanical power, irrigation facilities and farm implements etc. enhance male farmers active participation and adoption of different soil and water conservation structures during the implementation stage.

Risk preference of rural male farmers was observed highly positively and significantly correlated with their participation in implementation of the soil and water conservation programme. Farmers with higher risk preference are usually oriented towards maximization of income from agriculture. They adopt different new soil and water conservation structures on their land even at high cost. They have risk taking ability and are capable to contribute labour and money to project implementing agency during the construction of new SWC structures on their field and the land owned by the community. This ensures increase of sustainable agriculture production even from degraded and sloppy lands.

Level of knowledge among rural male farmers regarding soil and water conservation technologies was also observed highly positively and significantly correlated with males' participation in implementation of the soil and water conservation programme. It is a fact that if male farmers have improved knowledge level regarding soil and water conservation technologies they are capable of utilizing that knowledge for effective participation in implementation of soil and water conservation structures on their land. It would help generate more income.

If male farmers keep more favourable attitude towards soil and water conservation programme they may allow the project implementing authority to go ahead with implementation of soil and water conservation programme on their land. They might also impart substantial contribution to participation and in the form of labour and money to help implementation of soil and water conservation programme in their village.

It was also revealed that any increase in the age of male farmers decreased their participation in implementation non-significantly. Whereas any increase in the land holding, education, farm power, family size, income, social participation and adoption increases their participation in implementation of the soil and water conservation programme.

It was found that the age plays a negative and non-significant role as correlated with participation of male farmers in implementation of soil and water conservation programme. It was because of such fact that old rural male farmers have weak physical capabilities and are unable to perform tasks for effective participation. The old farmers are unable to contribute their own labour in implementation of soil and water conservation structures. Young farmers are physically strong enough to do hard work during construction of SWC structures on their field. Old farmers are unable to do hard work. The only thing that they can do is to share their experiences with young family members and other farmers.

Large size of land holding is conducive to adoption of different SWC structures. But the adoption of SWC technologies also depends on the condition, the type of soil, and the slope of land.

Educated male farmers possess little experience of working in agricultural fields. It might be because educated young male farmers are more interested in government jobs and businesses rather than to go for agriculture cultivation as their main occupation. Educated farmers in spite of knowledge, lack in practical skills to carry out different agricultural functions. They are out of the habit of working hard in fields. Therefore, they are unable to contribute their own labour and skill during the construction of SWC structures on their fields and that of the community land.

With large families in villages, male farmers may get a chance to involve them in soil and water conservation works and in adoption of different soil and water conservation structures. It is also a fact that most decisions in implementation and adoption of SWC structures are taken by head of the family.

Farmers may need huge finance for adoption and construction of soil and water conservation structures in their fields. But they are unable to afford high initial cost in adoption of SWC structures.

Rural male farmers who have more contacts with officials of rural village institutions and extension agencies can contribute effectively participation in planning and during implementation of SWC programme. Farmers expressed desire that the expenses required for construction of SWC structures on their fields and community land should be contributed from the government money through the Project Implementing Agency.

Adoption behaviour of rural male farmers regarding soil and water conservation technologies was observed as factor positively and non-significantly correlated with males' participation in implementation of the soil and water conservation programme. It is also a fact that if rural male farmers have already adopted soil and water conservation technologies on their land, they are likely to participate very little in implementation or adoption of soil and water conservation structures on their land. Due to early adoption of SWC structures on farmers' field, the land might be already levelled and managed properly. Hence, the land does not need any more construction or adoption of SWC structures.

**Relationship between the females' participation in implementation of soil and water conservation programme and selected independent variables:**

The study revealed that any increase in the socio-economic status, education, family size, social participation, risk preference, knowledge and attitude towards SWC programme affects increased participation of female farmers in implementation of soil and water conservation programme. Whereas, any increase in the age and income of female farmers affects decrease in their participation in implementation of soil and water conservation programme.

Socio-economic status of rural female farmers operates as factor highly positively and significantly correlated with their participation in implementation of the soil and water conservation programme. It indicates that rural female farmers with high level of socio-economic status participate more by contributing equipment, materials, machinery and money in implementation of SWC programme and also through actual adoption of practices.

Education among rural female farmers was found to be highly positively and significantly correlated with their participation in implementation of the SWC programme. The reasons might be that educated female farmers in rural areas are capable of supporting and help their spouses in their decisions related to farming. They can also help in making their families financially sound with additional income from their side. Educated women help male farmers also in budgeting and planning of agricultural resources. They, thus, support their spouses to affect increase in agricultural production by adopting SWC measures.

The size of a family works as a probable reason for positive and significant correlation of female farmers' participation in implementation of the soil and water conservation programme. The more is the number of persons in a family, the higher would be rural women's involvement and participation in implementation of the soil and water conservation programme. Large sized families have yet one more advantage in the form of more helping hands in agricultural operations. This allows female farmers to spare themselves for soil and water conservation works and hand over household tasks to other family members. They may also put to use the labour work contributed by their family members in implementation of SWC structures on their agricultural fields.

Female farmers in villages who have more contacts with rural village institutions and extension agencies can keep abreast of the latest innovations regarding soil and water conservation. They can also utilize that knowledge in implementation of the SWC programme. They can also offer help and guidance to other farmers, as and when needed, to affect proper implementation of different soil and water conservation structures on their land and that of community. They may also allow easy participation of labour and money.

Risk preference of rural female farmers was observed as highly positively and significantly correlated with females' participation in implementation of the soil and water conservation programme. It is a noteworthy fact that the higher risk preferred rural female farmers are oriented towards maximization of income from agriculture and they do it by adopting different soil and water conservation structures on their land.

If female farmers in villages have better knowledge level regarding soil and water conservation technologies, they can utilize that knowledge during implementation phase of the SWC programme. The highly knowledgeable women can contribute with more guidance and suggestions during implementation of soil and water conservation structures on their land as well as on that of the community land. It ensures sustainable agricultural production and generates more income.

Attitude of rural female farmers towards soil and water conservation programme was also observed highly positively and significantly correlated with their participation in implementation of soil and water conservation programme. It might be due to more favourable attitude of female farmers towards soil and water conservation programme, which is likely to allow project implementing authority to implement soil and water conservation programme on their land. They might also contribute more significantly by motivating other fellow farmers to adopt soil and water conservation structures on their land.

It was again revealed that factors like age and income were negatively and significantly correlated with female farmers' participation in implementation of the soil and water conservation programme. The fact remains that old rural female farmers are physically weak and have lower capacity for hard tasks. This unable them to contribute with hard labour work efficiently in their agricultural fields during implementation phase of the soil and water conservation programme with adoption of conservation structures. Old women in villages remain busy in rearing their children in the day time. Hence, all the decisions regarding contribution of labour and money in adoption of new SWC technologies remain with males in the family.

Similarly, the rich female farmers are not really interested to undertake agricultural works. They attach to it the point of view of their prestige in the society. They hire labourers on their farms and get the work done. These works include land levelling, bunding, summer ploughing, mulching, weeding, harvesting etc. Rich female farmers hire even poor labourers from outside to carry out their household works such as cutting of fodder, supply of fodder to animals, cutting of fuel wood for kitchen and threshing of cereals and pulses for home etc. It is generally noticed that rich female farmers in rural area are much bothered about their status and prestige in the society.

The study also revealed that any increase in the land holding, farm power affects adoption the participation of female farmers in implementation of soil and water conservation programme. It as such increases non-significantly.

The fact that the large sizes of land holdings usually have undulating topography and are also slopy. Hence, they are conducive and suitable for adoption of different soil and water conservation structures on their land.

The farm powers such as animal power, mechanical power, irrigation facilities and farm implements etc. help women's participation and adoption of different soil and water conservation structures, yet it was observed non-significant. The reasons might be that female farmers generally do not have any practice or skill to operate various farm powers and machinery such as various kind of ploughs, tube-well operation, use of bullock cart, tractor driving etc.

Adoption behaviour of rural female farmers towards soil and water conservation technologies was found to be positively and non-significantly correlated with female's participation in implementation of the soil and water conservation programme. The fact remains that rural female farmers with already more adoption of soil and water conservation practices are likely to have little intention for participation in implementation by over-adoption of soil and water conservation technologies.

## 4.10 RELATIONSHIP BETWEEN THE PARTICIPATION IN MAINTENANCE AND VARIABLES

**Relationship between the males' participation in maintenance of soil and water conservation programme and selected independent variables:**

The study revealed that any increase in the socio-economic status, land holding, farm power, family size, risk preference, knowledge, attitude and adoption of SWC practices helps to increase the participation of male farmers in maintenance of soil and water conservation programme.

The male farmers with more agricultural resources such as implements, materials, animal power, machinery etc. are capable of maintaining and repairing SWC structures constructed on their farm land. The farmers with more resources can easily contribute their resources to maintenance and repair of damaged SWC structures on the land owned by the community in a watershed area. The SWC structures can be damaged or breached due to heavy rain. In such situation, if a farmer has adequate farm implements and machinery he could arrange for the repair of the structures immediately and prevent any severe loss.

The male farmers with large size of land holdings are interested in maintaining the different SWC structures constructed on their land. It is because of the regular maintenance and repair of conservation structures, the fertility of the land is maintained, as well as the soil degradation and erosion are checked on considerable ground. It is, therefore, very important to maintain big size of land holdings to ensure sustainable agricultural production. Otherwise soil erosion may convert a cultivable land into an eroded land.

Farm power owned by rural male farmers was observed positively and significantly correlated with males' participation in maintenance of the soil and water conservation programme. Farm powers such as animal power, mechanical power, irrigation facilities and farm implements etc. help male farmers to carry out maintenance and repair work of damaged or breached different soil and water conservation structures on their field.

Large families in the form of the joint family system help the rural male farmers to have more helping hands in maintenance and repair of damaged soil and water conservation structures on their fields. Soil and water conservation structures are usually affected by various kinds of soil erosion throughout the year. Therefore, maintenance and repair of conservation structures is essential to derive proper benefits from the structures.

Male farmers in villages who keep higher risk preference are oriented towards maximization of income from agriculture. They repair the soil and water conservation structures on their land the moment they are damaged or breached. They do not neglect it, because it affects their benefits of increasing agricultural production with due conservation of soil and water. Hence, the risk taking ability helps farmers to maintain SWC structures to ensure sustainable agricultural production.

If male farmers in villages have better knowledge of soil and water conservation technologies, they know when and how to repair and maintain soil and water conservation structures on their land. Their awareness helps them increase sustainable agricultural production by maintaining fertility of soil and by conservation of natural nutrients due to siltation. Male farmers with good skills can easily carry out the repair of the SWC structures on their own when required.

Again, if male farmers hold more favourable attitude towards the soil and water conservation programme they hold strong feeling that the soil and water conservation programme has to be developed by the farmers, for the farmers and of the farmers. Hence, favourable attitude of farmers might help for good contribution of labour and money in the repair and maintenance of soil and water conservation structures on their land as well as on pasture land in the watershed of the community.

Rural male farmers, who have more adoption of the soil and water conservation technologies, are likely to maintain and repair soil and water conservation structures on their land to ensure sustainable agricultural production. Once th SWC structures are adopted on the field, it becomes necessary to repair and maintain them whenever they are damaged and breached. Such care would ensure long-term benefits from them.

It was also revealed that with the increase in the age, income and social participation have direct bearing on the participation of male farmers in maintenance of soil and water conservation programme. But it increases non-significantly. Whereas, with increase in education, the participation of male farmers in maintenance of soil and water conservation programme decreases non-significantly.

Old male farmers are weak in physical capacity. They are unable to contribute labour in maintenance of the SWC structures on their land as well as on the land owned by the community. Old farmers may also have feelings that they have done enough work in their young age and so now it is their turn to take rest in the old age. They think that young of their family should work in the field. They also want that the young members should learn about various SWC and agricultural practices, their maintenance and doing actual work with them in fields. Old age farmers have poor health and so they are unable to do hard work in field and carry out repair and maintenance of damaged SWC structures on their land.

Educaton among rural male farmers was found negatively and non-significantly correlated with their participation in maintenance of SWC programme. It is obvious that eduated male farmers have less experience of working in fields as they devote most of their time to study. It is also true that the educated young male farmers are more interested in jobs and businesses rather than to take up cultivation as occupation. It might be becausemost of the educated farmers accept jobs or businesses as their occupation. Because of it that again they do not gain much experience about agriculture and cultivation as well as soil and water conservation practices. With lack of experience on fields, educated farmers are unable to contribute with not enough participation in repair and maintenance of the SWC structures on their farm and that of the community.

Rich farmers can easily afford the cost required for repair and maintenance of the SWC structures. But most of them keep their land in good condition and levelled, hence there is very low cost to be incurred on repair and maintenance of the SWC structures on their farm. The rich farmers also prefer to get the repair and maintenance work done by hired labourers. They avoid doing any labour work themselves on their fields, as it would affect their prestige in their village and the society.

The rural male farmers who maintain more contacts with officials of rural village institutions and extension agencies are also likely to contribute more effectively in participation in maintenance of SWC programme. If these farmers adopt SWC structures on their lands for soil and water conservation, in that case the farmers manage their structures. It is necessary for them to get economic benefits from the structures even without more social participation.

## Relationship between the females' participation in maintenance of soil and water conservation programme and selected independent variables:

The present study revealed a fact that any increase in the socio-economic status, land holding, education, family size, risk preference, knowledge, attitude and adoption of SWC practices would help to allow increased participation of female farmers in maintenance of soil and water conservation programme.

The rural female farmers with high level of socio-economic status can manage more equipments, materials, machinery, money etc. which might be used properly in maintenance and repair of SWC structures to ensure sustainable agricultural production.

The large size of land holdings have undulating topography. Thus, they are conducive and more suitable for adoption of different soil and water conservation structures on their land. Once the SWC structures are adopted by female farmers it becomes necessary after that to maintain the conservation structures for control of soil erosion and sustainable production.

Educated female farmers in rural areas might help their spouses in proper decision making, and in making their families financially sound with increase in their income. Educated women motivate and advise their spouses to undertake timely repair and maintenance of adopted SWC structures. They possess more knowledge about maintenance of SWC structures.

It was found that the level of women's participation in maintenance increases with increase in the size of their families. The probable reason for above finding might be that with more persons in a family, rural women might get a chance to involve themselves with contribution of labour work and guidance in repair of damaged soil and water conservation structures. The large families enjoy advantage of having more helping hands to share the work of repair and maintenance of soil and water conservation structures adopted at their farm and that of the community. They can spare themselves for maintenance of soil and water conservation works after entrusting household activities to other members in their families.

Risk preference of rural female farmers was observed as factor positively and significantly correlated with their participation in maintenance of soil and water conservation programme. It is because of this that the higher risk preferred rural female farmers are oriented towards maximization of income from agriculture. They ensure timely repair and maintenance of various adopted soil and water conservation structures on their land. The female farmers are again ready to take risk in maintenance of structures for the interest of increasing their income.

Female farmers in villages with higher knowledge level regarding soil and water conservation technologies are capable of utilizing their knowledge during repair of damaged soil and water conservation structures on their land as well as on the land owned by the community. It ensures sustainable agricultural production for long time. Knowledgeable female farmers can also help their spouses in taking decisions during repair and maintenance of the SWC structures.

If female farmers have more favourable attitude towards the soil and water conservation programme they might develop good contacts with the staff of project implementing agncy. It helps them to learn about repair and maintenance of soil and water conservation structures on their land. They might even contribute more meaningfully in maintenance of the SWC structures on their farm as well as on that of the community land.

The rural female farmers who have adopted soil and water conservation technologies on their land might necessarily look to maintain and repair the soil and water conservation structures on their land to ensure sustainable agricultural production. It is also true that without proper care and maintenance of adopted conservation structures, their utility gets reduced and lost and money spent in their adoption will be a mere waste. Therefore, it is essential that the adopted structures should be maintained properly for their sustainable output for long period.

It was also revealed that with the increase in age and income, participation of female farmers in maintenance of soil and water conservation programme decreased non-significantly. Whereas, with increase in farm power and social participation, the participation of female farmers in maintenance of soil and water conservation programme increased non-significantly.

It was again revealed that the age is negatively and significantly correlated with participation in maintenance by female farmers in soil and water conservation programme. Old female farmers are physically weak and unable to contribute hard labour efficiently on their agricultural fields. They are unable to carry out so effectively the repair and maintenance of soil and water conservation structures. They usually remain busy in rearing their children in the day time.

Farm power owned by rural female farmers was observed positively and non-significantly correlated with females' participation in maintenance of soil and water conservation programme. The possible reasons might be that female farmers generally do not have adequate skill or knowledge to operate various farm power machinery such as various kind of ploughs, use of bullock cart, tractor driving etc.

Rich female farmers do not like to work themselves for the repair of soil and water conservation structures on their land. They see it affecting their prestige in the society. Usually they get the labour work done by hired labourers on their farms. It is also rue that rich male farmers do not allow their ladies to involve themselves in labour work on agricultural fields.

Social participation of rural female farmers is observed positively and non-significantly correlated with their participation in maintenance of the soil and water conservation programme. The reason is that when male farmers wanted to carry out any repair of damaged soil and water conservation structures in rural area or learn about it, they contact officials of project implementing agency and extension agencies easily, rather than female farmers. If rural female farmers have more contacts with rural village institutions and extension agencies they remain in contact with latest innovations regarding soil and water conservation. But due to gender problem they can explore fewer contactsthan the male farmers do.

## 4.11 RELATIONSHIP BETWEEN THE PEOPLE'S PARTICIPATION IN SWC PROGRAMME AND THE VARIABLE GENDER

The present study revealed that the variable gender was negatively and non-significantly correlated with people's overall participation and in implementation stage of the soil and water conservation programme. Whereas, gender was found positively and also non-significantly correlated with people's participation in planning and maintenance stages of the soil and water conservation programme.

It was revealed that the independent variable gender does not have significant correlation with different dependent variables of people's participation in SWC programme. It is due to the fact that both the male and female respondents are participating in cultivation works on their fields. Therefore, no difference is noticed between the participation of male respondents and female respondents in the light of an overall extent of people's participation and in different stages of the Antisar watershed development programme such as planning, implementation and maintenance. Thus, the female respondents contributed equally as the male respondents, and vise-versa, when their participation in the soil and water conservation programme is counted. Hence, both the male and female farmers can be involved in the soil and water conservation programme on watershed basis on equal ground.

## 4.12 CONSTRAINTS FACED BY RESPONDENTS

It was revealed from the study that majority of the male respondents faced some constraints during Antisar watershed development programme. They included lack of finance, high cost involved in adoption of technology, shortage of labour in watershed area, lack of knowledge about watershed management practices, inadequate transport facilities and lack of cooperation of people.

Similarly, majority of the female respondents also faced the constraints during Antisar watershed development programme, such as lack of finance, shortage of labour in watershed, high cost involved in adoption of technology, lack of knowledge about watershed management practices, lack of cooperation of people and inadequate transport facilities.

Such problems include that farmers of Antisar watershed face shortage of money for adoption of costly SWC structures. Since, the majority of rural male and female farmers have land holdings and majority of farmers having cultivation of their main occupation. Therefore, there was non-availability of landless labourers for agriculture occupation. It is also due to that the rich farmers do not like to work in their fields because of their prestige point in the society. There was also non-availability of institution in nearby area to guide the farmers about soil and water conservation technologies. The Antisar watershed is in rural area and there is also lack of transport facilities.

The implication for the above findings is that:

- Loan facilities should be provided in rural area to meet the initial cost involved in adoption of the SWC structures.
- Farmers should be motivated to do labour work on their on farm.
- Low cost or no cost technologies should be developed.
- Skilled trainings for target group farmers should be organized to improve the awareness among the farmers regarding SWC technologies.
- Farmers should be motivated to cooperate with each other during the adoption of SWC technologies.

## 4.13 CRITERIA FOR PARTICIPATORY APPROACH IN WATERSHED MANAGEMENT

The following criteria for appropriate participatory approach for sustainable agricultural production in watershed management are suggested on the basis of the findings and discussion of the study:

1. Middle age and young age rural male and female farmers should be given priority in such soil and water conservation development programmes on watershed basis.
2. Efforts should be made to increase the social participation of rural female farmers. They should be encouraged to be members of village level organizations or take up any position in the Panchayat. Such assignments will motivate them for more frequent contacts to local organization and participation in meetings.
3. Approach of collective farming on watershed basis may be adopted for sustainable agricultural production.
4. Farmers should be motivated to maintain adequate farm power viz. implements, machines etc. they are helpful in the soil and water conservation works.
5. Efforts should be made so that the farmers may develop in their character risk taking ability. It may help them to adopt new soil and water conservation technologies and derive maximum benefits from them with increase in agriculture production, fertility of land and increase in income on long term basis.

6. Skill oriented training programme should be organized by experts at village level for both male and female farmers, during watershed development programme. Such programmes will improve their knowledge regarding improved soil and water conservation technologies.

7. Bottom-up approach should be adopted in soil and water conservation programme on watershed basis. It means that the soil and water conservation programme should be developed by the rural farmers, for the farmers and of the farmers.

8. Need-based programme: The basic needs of the rural farmers' viz., fuel, fodder and food should be taken care of through the planning of the SWC programme. It encourages among local farmers for more favourable attitude towards the SWC programmes.

9. Low cost soil and water conservation technologies that may suit most to marginal and small land holdings should be disseminated to farmers for easy adoption.

10. Planning meetings of watershed development committee members, Users groups and self-help groups should be organized on regular basis to plan the watershed development activities systematically.

11. Local village leader should be identified. They have good influence over local farmers. A leader should properly appraise the soil and water conservation programme to the people of his village and organize watershed development programmes through committees for action. He would form a team of young and skilled farmers and lead them into action.

12. People of villages should be otivated for participation in the SWC programme. They may be encouraged to contribute their own labour, money, implements and materials in construction of soil and water conservation structures during implementation stage of the programme.

13. Farmers have tendency to be dependent more on the government or project implementing agency. Therefore, they should be taught to become self-reliant. They may receive guidance and technical assistance from government and project implementing agencies. But development of watershed programme has to be through their participation in labour and monetary contribution.

14. Attempts should be made through an agency like watershed development society so that the male and female farmers become aware and alert about their rights, privileges, duties and responsibilities in matters of repair and maintain the soil and water conservation practices adopted on watershed basis. Such attempts ensure proper care of SWC structures even after the project is accomplished by PIA.

15. The farmers should be motivated for proper maintenance and repair of SWC structures by contributing their own labour and money. It would go in the interest of sustainable agricultural production.

# CITED LITERATURE

1. Anonymous (1994). Guidelines for Watershed Development, Ministry of Rural Development, Govt. of India, PP:1.

2. Anonymous (1998). Soil and Water Conservation Annual Report 1997-98, Central Soil & Water Conservation Research & Training Institute, Dehradun, pp: 1-2.

3. Banki, Evan S. (1981). Dictionary of Administration and Management. Los Angeles, California: Systems Research Institute, pp: 533.

4. Cohen, John, M. and Uphoff, Norman, T. (1980). "Participation's place in rural development seeking clarity through specificity", world development, 8(3), pp: 213-236.

5. FAO, (1989). Sustainable Development Natural Resources Management, Twenty Fifth Conference Paper C 89/2-Sup.2, Rome, Italy.

6. Hunter, Guy. (1980). "Linking levels of planning and action for participatory rural development" Rural Development Participation Review, 1(3), pp: 5-7.

7. Jose, P.D. (1994). "Participation management of development programmes" Journal of Rural Development, Vol. 13, No.4, pp. 515-525.

8. Karl Deutsch (1969). "Social mobilization and political development, American political science review, L IV.

9. Khatik, G.L., Kumar, V., Singh, H.B. & Pande, V.C. (1998). "People's participation in soil and water conservation programmes in Mahi ravines", Indian Journal of Extension Education, Vol. 34 Nos. 3&4, pp: 100-103.

10. Mishra, S.N., Sharma, K. and Sharma, N. (1984). Participation and Development, Delhi: NBO Publishers' Distributors, pp: 17-29.

11. Mishra, Y. (1994). People's participation in production process under watershed, Kurukshetra. 42, 11, August; pp: 25-27.

12. Moulik, T.K. (1978). "Techniques of mobilizing rural people to support rural development programme", in APDAC, Rural Development: Training to meet new Challenges, Vol. 4, Kuala Lumpur.

13. Muthayya, B.C. (1973). "Psychological aspects of community development", community development and Panchayati Raj Digest, 5(2), 00-07, NIRD, Hyderabad.

14. Paroda, R.S. (2000). From the DG's Desk, ICAR Reporter, Indian Council of Agricultural Research, Krishi Anusandhan Bhavan, Pusa, New Delhi, April-June 2000, pp: 1-2.

15. Peabody, R.L. (1965). "Public Bureaucracies", in J.G. March, (ed.) Handbook of Organizations, New York.

16. Santhanam, M.L., Yogananda Sastry, C. and Vijayakumar, S. (1982). " Human and social factors in people's participation", Journal of Rural Development, Vol. 1, No. 5, PP: 770-831.

17. Sharma, Sudesh, K. (1979). "People's Participation in Integrated Rural Development", In: Arora R.K. (ed.) People's Participation in Development Process, The HCM State.

18. Singh, R.B. (1990). Sustainable agriculture Issues, Perspectives and Prospects in Semi-Ard Tropics, Proceedings of the First International Symposium on Natural Resources Management for a Sustainable Agriculture, Indian Society of Agronomy, New Delhi, pp: 279-280.

19. Singh, R.P. (1993). "Dryland agriculture and technological options: Issues and approaches for watershed development," Journal of Rural Development, Vol. 12(1), PP: 21-33.

20. Singh, R.P., Sharma, P., Padmanahbam,M.V., Das, S.K. and Mishra, P.K. (1990). Field manual on watershed management, Central Research Institute for Dryland Agriculture, Hyderabad, India, pp: 134.

21. Swaminathan, M.S. (1998). The watershed concept, University News, Vol. 36, No.19, May 11, pp: 14-17.

22. Tyagi, L.K. (1998) People's participation in rural development, Employment News, Vol. XXIII, No.11, pp. 1-2.

23. Verhagen, Koenroad, (1980). "How to promote people's participation in rural development through local organizations", Review of International Cooperation, 73(1), pp: 28.

24. Yadav, Ram. P. (1980). "People's participation: Focus on mobilization of the rural poor", in UNAPDI, local level planning: Alternative strategy, Concept Publishing Co., New Delhi.

# BIBLIOGRAPHY

1. Best, J.W. and Kahn, J.V. (1999). Research in Education, Seventh Edition, Prentice Hall of India, New Delhi, pp: 302-307.

2. Bhatt, S.R. (1990). Transfer of Hybrid Maize Technology Among the Tribal Farmers of Girwa Block in Udaipur District of Rajasthan State. Unpublished M.Sc. (Agri.) Thesis, G.A.U., Anand.

3. Bhutiya, Khorla (1993). „A study on attitude of adopters and non-adopter farmers towards watershed management programme in Sikkim" M.Sc.(Agri.) Thesis Gujarat Agricultural University, S.K. Nagar.

4. Chaudhary, N.V., Prajapati, M.R. and Soni, M.C. (1996). „Knowledge and adoption of soil analysis practices by the farmers of Banaskantha district of Gujarat State, Gujarat Journal of Extension Education, 6&7: pp: 144-148.

5. Ferguson, G.A. 1981. Statistical analysis in psychology and education (fifth edition). New York: McGraw-Hill, pp: 419-432.

6. Gamit, S.S. (1993). A study of Extent of Adoption of Recommended Summer Groundnut Technology by the Tribal Farmers of Panchmahals District of Gujarat State. Unpublished M.Sc. Thesis, G.A.U., Sardar Krushinagar.

7. Ingole, N.P. Saigaonkar, P.B. and Kothekar M.D. (1993). Television viewing behaviour of farmers, Indian Journal of Extension Education, Vol. XXIX, Nos. 3&4, PP: 54-55.

8. Kerlinger, F.N. (1976). Foundation of Behavioural Research, New Delhi. Surjee Publication: 198-204.

9. Kulkarni, M.V. and Nandapurkar, G.G. (1991). "Participation of rural women in decision making" Maharashtra Journal of Extension Education, Vol.X, No.2, pp: 307-308.

10. Nandrana, S.M. (1994). "A study on farmers' knowledge about well recharge practices", A special problem Department of Extension Education, College of Agriculture, GAU, Junagarh.

11. Padmaiah, M. et al. (1997). "Determinants of Awareness, Knowledge, Attitude and Adoption Behaviour of Farmers of Integrated Watershed Development Programme", Indian Journal of Soil Conservation, Vol. 25, No.3, pp: 250-252.

12. Padmaiah, H., Rao, M.S., R.M. Chittaranjan, S. and Salvarajan, S. (1992). "Impact of Watershed management programme on knowledge, attitude and adoption behaviour of farmers in Jaldarsi watershed of Bellary district, Karnataka", Indian Journal of Soil Conservation, 20 (1&2): pp: 37-43.

13. Pareek, U. & Trivedi, G. (1963). "Factor analysis of socio-economic status of farmers in India", Rural Sociology, 30, pp: 311-321.

14. Patel, N.R. (1991). "Dynamic of adoption of new agricultural technology and consequences in watershed area of Banaskantha and Mehsana district of Gujarat". Ph.D. thesis, Gujarat Agricultural University, S.K. Nagar.

15. Prabhu, M.K.K. and Kadam, K.S. (1990). "A study on knowledge level of farmers towards soil conservation practices", Indian Journal of Extension Education, 25 (3&4), pp: 86-88.

16. Rakholia, P.M. (1996). "Impact of watershed development Programme, M.Sc. (Agri.) Thesis, Gujarat Agricultural University, S.K. Nagar.

17. Reddy, H.C.V. (1987). "Attitude and adoption behaviour of farmers relating to watershed development programme in Bangalore district. M.Sc.(Agri.) Thesis, University of Agricultural Science, Bangalore.

18. Sen, D; Purandare, A.P. and Das, P.K. (1986). "People's participation in community forestry. A case study in Maharashtra", Journal of Rural Development, Vol.5, No.2, PP: 172.

19. Singh, A.K; Sharma, J.S. and Singh, D.K. (1988). "Participation of rural farm women in Agriculture in the hills of Uttar Pradesh". Journal of Rural Development, Vol. 7 No.3, PP: 289-297.

20. Suresh, K.A. (1990). "Participation of beneficiaries in the development programmes of non-Governmental organizations in Kerala" Journal of Rural Development, Vol. 9, No.5, PP: 911-915.

21. Trivedi, J.C. (1984). Transfer of Agricultural Technology Among Tribal Farmers of Panchmahals District - Gujarat State'. Unpublished Ph.D. Thesis, G.A.U., Anand.

22. Varma, S.K. and Sinha, B.P. (1992). "Involvement of Women and Men in Cultivation of Crops" Indian Journal of Extension Education, Vol. XXVIII, Nos. 3&4, pp: 49-55.

# APPENDIX

Interview schedule for the research study entitled "people's participation in soil and water conservation for sustainable agricultural production in Antisar watershed"

## INTERVIEW SCHEDULE

1. **Sr. No.** _____
2. **Date of interview** _____
3. **Name of respondent** _____
4. **Gender:**
   Male _____
   Female _____
5. **Name of village** _____
6. **Age of respondent** _____ years
7. **Socio-economic status scale:**
   (Please furnish the following information)

| Items | Scores |
|---|---|
| **I. Size of family land holding (acres):** | |
| Irrigated | _____ |
| Unirrigated | _____ |
| Total | _____ |
| **II. Education:** | |
| Illiterate | 0 |
| Can read only | 1 |
| Can read & write | 2 |
| Primary | 3 |
| Secondary | 4 |
| Higher Secondary | 5 |
| Graduate | 6 |
| Above graduate | 7 |
| **III. House:** | |
| No own house/rented | 0 |
| Own hut | 1 |
| Own kutcha house | 2 |

| | |
|---|---|
| Own semi-pucca house | 3 |
| Own pucca house | 4 |
| Own mansion | 6 |

### IV. Occupation:

| | |
|---|---|
| Labour | 1 |
| Business | 2 |
| Cultivation | 3 |
| Service | 4 |

### V. Caste:

| | |
|---|---|
| Scheduled Caste | 1 |
| Scheduled Tribe | 2 |
| Backward caste | 3 |
| General caste | 4 |
| Dominant caste | 5 |

### VI. Farm powers:

**(a) Animal power:**

| Name of animal | **Numbers** |
|---|---|
| Bullock | _____ |
| Cow | _____ |
| Buffalo | _____ |
| **Total** | _____ |

**(b) Mechanical power:**

| | |
|---|---|
| Bullock cart | 1 |
| Tractor | 3 |
| Trailer | 2 |
| Jeep/Car | 2 |
| Motor cycle/scooter | 1 |
| Cycle | 1 |

**(c) Irrigation facilities:**

| | |
|---|---|
| Open well | 1 |
| Tube well | 2 |

| | |
|---|---|
| Canal | 1 |
| Pond | 1 |
| Diesel pump set | 1 |
| Electric pump set | 2 |

**(d) Farm implements:**

| | |
|---|---|
| Country plough | 1 |
| Mould board plough | 1 |
| Disc harrow | 1 |
| Cultivator | 1 |
| Puddler | 1 |
| Harrow | 1 |
| Thresher | 1 |
| Winnower | 1 |
| Duster | 1 |
| Sprayer | 1 |
| Seed drill | 1 |
| Chaff cutter | 1 |

**VII. Material possessions:**

| | |
|---|---|
| Chair | 1 |
| Table | 1 |
| Sofa set | 2 |
| Steel/Wooden almirah | 1 |
| Radio | 1 |
| Sewing machine | 1 |
| Electric fan | 1 |
| Tape recorder | 1 |
| Television | 2 |
| Refrigerator | 2 |

**VIII (a)**                                                           **Family Type:**

(i)    Nuclear family                                              ———

(ii)   Joint family                                                   ———

| (b) Family size: | |
|---|---|
| (a) Number of male family members | _____ |
| (b) Number of female family members | _____ |
| (d) Total family members | _____ |

**IX. Annual income of family in rupees:**

| | |
|---|---|
| Upto Rs. 25,000 | 1 |
| Rs. 25,001 to Rs. 50,000 | 2 |
| Rs. 50,001 to Rs. 75,000 | 3 |
| Rs. 75,001 to Rs. 1,00,000 | 4 |
| Above Rs. 1,00,000 | 5 |

**8. Social participation:**

a) Have you ever been a member/office-bearer of any rural organization? Yes/No

b) If yes, please give the following particulars.

| Sr. No. | Name of organization | Member | | Office-bearer | |
|---|---|---|---|---|---|
| | | Past | Present | Past | Present |
| | Score | 1 | 2 | 3 | 4 |
| 1. | Panchayat member | | | | |
| 2. | Milk producers cooperative society | | | | |
| 3. | Multipurpose cooperative society | | | | |
| 4. | Youth club | | | | |
| 5. | Religious organization | | | | |
| 6. | Political organization | | | | |
| 7. | Any other (specify) | | | | |

**9. Risk preference:**

Please give your responses as agree, undecided and disagree by putting tick mark (3) towards all the statements. The scores for positive statements were as 3 for agree; 2 for ndecided and 1 for disagree and the reverse scores were assigned for negative statements. Where; A. = Agree, U.D. = Undecided and D.A. = Disagree.

| Sr. No. | Statements | A. | U.D. | D.A. |
|---|---|---|---|---|
| 1. | You would prefer to adopt new Soil and Water Conservation (SWC) technologies for production in degraded wasteland. | | | |
| 2. | You would prefer to grow more crops than one in order to avoid total failure of crop. | | | |
| 3. | You would like to adopt SWC technologies in cultivable land at any cost for increasing production. | | | |
| 4. | You would try new Soil and Water Conservation methods only after most farmers have used them successfully. | | | |
| 5. | You would like to try an entirely new SWC technology in farming that involves higher financial investment but it is highly productive. | | | |
| 6. | You would like to adopt Soil and Water Conservation methods only, when you know the surety of successful agricultural production. | | | |
| 7. | You would prefer to try new SWC technology irrespective of it being successful or failure. | | | |
| 8. | You would like to continue with old technologies than adopting new SWC technologies about which you are not sure/confident. | | | |
| 9. | Even if you failed in adoption of new SWC technology first time, you would still like to try it once more. | | | |
| 10. | You would like to adopt new SWC technology only after the technology successfully demonstrated results at government research farm. | | | |

**10. A scale to measure knowledge level of rural farmers regarding soil and water conservation technologies:**

Please give your response as tick mark (3) in the column Yes or No against each practice of SWC according to your understanding. The correct response will be given score 1 and incorrect response will be given score 0.

| Sr.No. | Statements | Responses | |
|---|---|---|---|
| | | Yes | No |
| 1. | The materials such as saw dust, straw, paddy husk, groundnut shell, crop residues, leaves etc. are spread on the surface of the land to protect the soil from erosion. | | |
| 2. | The two or more crops are grown simultaneously for continuous land cover and protection from beating action of rains. | | |
| 3. | The crops with less canopy cover are grown to protect the soil from rain water erosion. | | |
| 4. | The crops are grown across the slope of the agriculture field. | | |
| 5. | The crops are grown along the slope of the land. | | |
| 6. | The cultivation of cereal crops is followed by pulse or leguminous crops. | | |
| 7. | In crop cultivation, cereal crops follow the cereal crops only. | | |
| 8. | The bunds are made along the slope of the sloppy land. | | |
| 9. | The trees are planted on the boundaries of crop fields. | | |
| 10. | The waterways used for conducting surface water in agricultural fields should not be covered with grasses. | | |
| 11. | The animals can be allowed in the specific grazing land after adequate growth of vegetation. | | |
| 12. | The minimum ploughing is done to create appropriate soil condition for seed germination. | | |
| 13. | One crop is grown repeatedly in cultivable land, year after year. | | |

14. In the fallow fields, the stubbles of crops are taken completely with roots.

11. A scale to measure attitude of people's participation towards SWC programme:

Please give your responses as agree, neutral and disagree by putting tick mark (3) towards all the statements. The scores for positive statements were as 3 for agree; 2 for neutral and 1 for disagree and the reverse scores were assigned for negative statements. Where; A. = Agree, N. = Neutral and D.A. = Disagree.

| Sr. No. | Statements | A. | N. | D.A. |
|---|---|---|---|---|
| | **A. Participation in programme planning:** | | | |
| 1. | Farmers should participate in soil & water conservation (SWC) programme planning meetings. | | | |
| 2. | Farmers should suggest any poit of individual or collective interest in planning of SWC programme. | | | |
| 3. | Women's participation in SWC programme planning meetings is inessential. | | | |
| | **B. Participation in programme implementation:** | | | |
| 4. | Farmers should contribute materials or equipments in construction of SWC structures. | | | |
| 5. | Farmers should contribute own labour or money in construction of SWC structures. | | | |
| 6. | Farmer's contribution of labour or money in construction of SWC structures is not required. | | | |
| 7. | SWC structures should be constructed by government money through project implementation agency (PIA). | | | |
| 8. | PIA is totally responsible for construction of SWC structures in farmer's fields. | | | |

| | **C. Participation in programme maintenance:** |
|---|---|
| 9. | Farmers should maintain and repair their SWC structures time to time by own expenses. |
| 10. | Farmers should contribute labour or money towards repair and maintenance of their SWC structures. |
| 11. | Farmers should motivate their fellow farmers for collectively contribution in repair and maintenance of SWC structures. |
| 12. | Maintenance and repair works should be done through PIA by government money. |
| 13. | Farmers should not contribute labour or money to the government body PIA for repair of SWC structures. |

**12. A scale to measure adoption behaviour of farmers towards SWC technologies:**

Please tick mark (✓) in appropriate column against each SWC technology on three-point-continuum of not known, known but not adopted and adopted. The weightages for responses of not known, known but not adopted and adopted were given as score 1, 2 and 3 respectively.

| Sr. No. | Technology | Responses | | |
|---|---|---|---|---|
| | | Not known | Known but not adopted | Adopted |
| 1. | Contour farming | | | |
| 2. | Intercropping | | | |
| 3. | Cover cropping | | | |
| 4. | Mulching | | | |
| 5. | Summer ploughing | | | |
| 6. | Land levelling | | | |
| 7. | Contour bunding | | | |
| 8. | Marginal bund | | | |

9. Terracing
10. Checkdam
11. Gully plug
12. Farm pond

13. Schedules to measure people's participation in various stages of soil and water conservation programme in watershed management.

Please give your response by tick mark (3) in appropriate column against each statement on three point-continuum as great extent (GE), some extent (SE) and least extent/never (LE/N). The weightages for responses of great extent, some extent and least extent were given as score 3, 2 and 1 respectively.

A. People's participation in programme planning stage:

| Sr. No. | Statements | GE | SE | LE/N |
|---|---|---|---|---|
| 1. | Did you participate in planning meeting of Soil and Water Conservation (SWC) programme? | | | |
| 2. | Have you suggested information to include in planning of soil and water conservation programme? | | | |
| 3. | Have you suggested any idea in the planning of agricultural crop cultivation in the watershed area? | | | |
| 4. | Have you suggested information during planning of various forest trees planted in the watershed? | | | |
| 5. | Have you suggested any idea during planning of land levelling works carried out in the different fields of the watershed area? | | | |
| 6. | Have you suggested any idea during planning of checkdam in the watershed? | | | |
| 7. | Did you participate in planning of various kinds of fruit plants grown in the watershed? | | | |
| 8. | Did you contact the Programme Implementing Agency (PIA) about your | | | |

primary needs such as fuel, fodder & food to be taken care of in the programme planning?

9. Do you motivate your fellow farmers to participate in planning of SWC programme?

10. Did you share any information or experience about soil and water conservation measures with your fellow farmers after participating in planning of conservation programme?

**B. People's participation in programme implementation stage:**

| Sr. No. | Statements | GE | SE | LE/N |
|---|---|---|---|---|
| 1. | Did you allow programme implementing agency (PIA) to implement soil and water conservation programme works in your field? | | | |
| 2. | Did you provide any material in the construction of soil and water conservation structures? | | | |
| 3. | Did you provide any equipment to the PIA during the construction of soil and water conservation measures in the watershed? | | | |
| 4. | Did you help during the plantation work of the fruit plants? | | | |
| 5. | Did you help in the plantation work of forest plants? | | | |
| 6. | Did you provide any help during purchasing of construction materials for soil and water conservation structures? | | | |
| 7. | Did you contribute any labour towards construction of soil and water conservation structures? | | | |
| 8. | Did you contribute any money towards construction of soil and water conservation structures? | | | |
| 9. | Did you ask your fellow resource users for labour and money contribution towards construction of conservation structures? | | | |

10. Did you participate in any training programme organized by the programme implementing agency regarding soil and water conservation programme?

## C. People's participation in programme maintenance stage:

| Sr. No. | Statements | GE | SE | LE/N |
|---|---|---|---|---|
| 1. | Do you protect the forest plantation done in the watershed area from the animals? | | | |
| 2. | Do you also protect the fruit plants grown in the watershed area? | | | |
| 3. | Do you take care of the forest plants and fruit plants during summer by providing irrigation water? | | | |
| 4. | Do you inform the PIA officers to repair the damaged soil and water conservation structures in the watershed? | | | |
| 5. | Do you contribute own labour towards repair and maintenance of soil and water conservation structure in your field? | | | |
| 6. | Do you contribute any money towards repair and maintenance of soil and water conservation structures in your field? | | | |
| 7. | Do you motivate your fellow farmers for labour contribution towards repair and maintenance of soil and water conservation structures in the watershed? | | | |
| 8. | Do you consult with the programme implementing agency to learn about repair and maintenance of conservation structures? | | | |
| 9. | Do you motivate your fellow farmers for money contribution towards repair and maintenance of soil and water conservation structures in the watershed? | | | |
| 10. | Do you protect the soil and water conservation structures from natural calamities? | | | |

14. **Constraints faced by you during the Antisar watershed development programme:**

Please tick mark (✓) against the constraints faced by you during the Antisar watershed development programme.

| Sr. No. | Constraints | Yes | No |
|---|---|---|---|
| | **(A) Economical Constraints:** | | |
| 1. | Lack of finance | | |
| 2. | High cost involved in adoption of technology | | |
| 3. | Lack of marketing facilities | | |
| | **(B) Technological Constraints:** | | |
| 4. | Lack of knowledge about watershed management practices. | | |
| 5. | Lack of technical guidance. | | |
| 6. | Complexity of technology | | |
| | **(C) Input Availability Constraints:** | | |
| 7. | Shortage of labour in watershed | | |
| 8. | Inadequate transport facilities | | |
| 9. | Inadequate availability of inputs needed | | |
| | **(D) Situational Constraints:** | | |
| 10. | Lack of good leadership in the watershed | | |
| 11. | Political interference | | |
| 12. | Lack of cooperation of people | | |
| 13. | Factionalism of population | | |

**Signature of interviewer**

# Index

## A

Adoption 28
  category 28
  of summer ploughing 84
  of SWC practices 24
  quotient 48
Agricultural
  cultivation 23, 144, 146
  innovations 27
  operations 143
Alternative development 11
Arid areas 21
Attitude 27, 47, 77
  levels of respondents 77
  of respondents 40
  towards SWC programme 27

## B

Barren land 21
Beneficiaries 15, 17, 22, 151, 179
Bibliography 178

## C

Cited Literature 176
Collection of data 42
Community
  Development Programme 12
  education 150
  forestry 150
Comprehensive 5
Conceived 8, 152
Concept
  of integrated treatment 4
  of participation 11
  of people's participation 11, 12
  of watershed 19
  of watershed management 22

Conservation
  for sustainable agricultural 20
  programme 19
  programmes 16, 17
  projects 6
  technologies 19, 24
Constraints
    22, 30, 41, 52, 53, 140
Counter development 11
Cropping intensity 4, 5, 9, 145

## D

Deforestation 21
Degradation 19, 21, 168
Development activities 36
Discussion
    38, 143, 149, 156, 173, 194

## E

Encouraged 8, 159, 173, 174
Environmental imbalance 21
Erosion rates 7
Exacerbate 5
Extension agencies
    153, 155, 160, 164, 166, 170, 172

## F

Feasibility 35
First Five Year Plan 11

## G

Gender
    23, 29, 30, 31, 38, 43, 52, 54, 138
gender variable 23
Green revolution technologies 9
Guidelines 36
Guidelines for strategies 36

## H

Holistic framework 4
Human personality 11

## I

Illiteracy 144
Incorporated 41, 148
Indiscriminate 9
Influential 152
Integrated treatment 4
Integrated watershed management 4
Interview method 35
Introduction 21
Investigator 23, 33, 35, 42, 45, 51

## J

Judicial utilization 21
Justification 22, 23

## L

Land degradati 21
Land degradation 21
Literacy rate 152
Local rural organizations 151
Locale of the study 34

## M

Methodology 34, 76
Moderate
  infrastructure 143
  level of participation
    86, 88, 90, 93, 96, 99, 105, 142, 151

## N

NWDPRA 6, 36

## O

Operational Research Projects 8

## P

Panchayati Raj System 12
Paroda 8
Participation 11
Participatory approach 143, 173, 19, 22, 30, 36, 173

Performance 12
Pilot study 35
Population
  of the study 36
Posterity 10
Poverty 144
Present status 7
Pressure on land 8
Prevalent 151
Project implementing agencies 22, 174

## R

Rainfed areas 4
Ravines 7, 8, 21, 176
Research Design 37
Rural reconstruction programme 11

## S

Significance 22
Social Participation 26, 44, 116, 136, 142, 153, 172

## T

Tendency 174
Tendency of taking risks 146
Tribal respondents 146

## U

Uncertainty 45, 146

## W

Watershed 3
  approach 3, 4
  concept 6
  development 4
  development agency 3
  development Programme
    in Rainfed Areas 6
  development programmes 1
  management 3, 5